Stop *Pretending*

Luis Palau

with Stephen and Amanda Sorenson

NE✗GEN®

An imprint of
Cook Communications Ministries

Nexgen ® is an imprint of
Cook Communications Ministries, Colorado Springs, Colorado 80918
Cook Communications, Paris, Ontario
Kingsway Communications, Eastbourne, England

STOP PRETENDING
Previously titled: *Time to Stop Pretending*
© 1985, 2003 by Luis Palau

First Printing (new edition), 2003
Printed in the United States of America

1 2 3 4 5 6 7 8 9 10 Printing/Year 10 09 08 07 06 05 04 03

Editor (over revision): Craig Bubeck, Senior Editor
Cover & Interior Design: Andrea L. Boven, Boven Design Studio, Inc.

If you have any questions or desire further information about the material presented in this book, please contact Luis Palau, President, Luis Palau Evangelistic Association, P.O. Box 1173, Portland, Oregon 97207, USA, (503) 614-1500, www.palau.org, lpea@palau.org.

All scripture quotations, unless otherwise indicateed, are taken from the HOLY BIBLE: NEW INTERNATIONAL VERSION®. NIV®. Copyright © 1973, 1978, 1984 by International Bible Society. Used by permission of Zondervan Publishing House. All rights reserved. Scripture quotations marked (NLT) are taken from the HOLY BIBLE, New Living Translation, copyright © 1996. Used by permission of Tyndale House Publishers, Inc., Wheaton, Illinois 60189.
Scripture marked (RSV), are from the *Revised Standard Version of the Bible*©, 1946, 1952, 1971, 1973 by Division of Chirstian Education of the National Council of Churches in the United Stated of America.
Scripture marked (KJV) are from the HOLY BIBLE, King James Version.

Library of Congress Cataloging-in-Publication Data

Palau, Luis, 1934-
  Stop pretending / Luis Palau with Stephen and Amanda Sorenson.
    p. cm.
  Rev. ed. of: Time to stop pretending. c1985.
  ISBN 0-7814-3892-6
  1. Bible. N.T. Corinthians, 2nd, I-VI--Sermons. 2. Sermons,
American--20th century. I. Sorenson, Stephen. II. Sorenson, Amanda,
1953- III. Palau, Luis, 1934- Time to stop pretending. IV. Title.
  BS2675.54 .P35 2003
  248.4--dc21

                                    2002151902

CONTENTS

If you're serious about life change, take this book off the shelf! Luis, thanks for showing me that the "authentic Christian life" is the good life!

—*Mike Silva, President, Mike Silva Evangelism, Inc.*

Luis Palau uses dynamic illustrations and a compelling story-telling style to illustrate the core issues of life. *Stop Pretending* will speak to your heart, opening the way for God to change it forever.

—*Dan Lagasse, Pastor of Global Outreach,*
Los Gatos Christian Church, Los Gatos, California

Stop Pretending captures the heart of one of the greatest Christian spokesmen of our generation. More than a 'self-help' book, Luis Palau takes us back to the Bible for the keys to successful Christian living. Prepare to be challenged. Expect to be encouraged.

—*Jose Zayas, President, Jose Zayas Evangelism, Inc.*

Luis Palau writes about real life, real struggles, and real issues in *Stop Pretending.* I was blessed to be mentored by Luis Palau for more than a dozen years and saw him live out these principles of walking with Christ. I appreciate his honesty, transparency, and the biblical insights he gives to help us be Christ-like. Those who are serious about being a truly devoted follower of Jesus Christ will want to read this book.

—*Daniel Owens, Evangelist and*
author of In God We Trust... But Only as a Last Resort

From the moment I picked up this book, I was glued to it. Luis does what he does best—he takes God's Word and brings it right into my world. This book called me to be real, honest, and authentic. I'm glad I read it!

—*William Wilson, Senior Pastor, Portland Christian Center,*
Portland, Oregon

To
Kevin,
Keith,
Andrew,
and Stephen

My family, fellow evangelistic team members, and other friends sometimes give me a hard time. "Hey, Luis," they say with a smile, "are you going to talk about the principles of authentic Christian living *again?*" They know from experience that I long to encourage believers to learn and apply biblical principles for living triumphantly in Christ.

Yes, my passion is to win as many people as possible to Jesus Christ. But that's only the beginning. I sincerely believe God has much more than salvation in store for each of His children. He wants us to enjoy the fact that He "always leads in triumph" every day of our lives.

I find it sad that many Christians around the world are not living authentic lives in Christ. Oh, they yearn to experience the full joy He promises, but they don't know how to fill the gaping hole in their Christian lives. This book explains how to fill that void.

If you're looking for an easy three-step formula for enjoying the Christian life, please look elsewhere. Victorious Christian living can't be manufactured or masqueraded. As the Apostle Paul reveals in the first half of 2 Corinthians, only God can produce it in us.

After preaching these messages for a number of years, I'm delighted to present them to you in written form. My special thanks to David L. Jones, David Sanford, James M. Williams, and the many other Luis Palau Evangelistic Association team members who helped with this project from start to finish, to Amanda and Stephen Sorenson for providing the extra help needed to make this book a reality, and to Renée S. Sanford for helping me prepare this new, updated edition.

PART ONE

The All-Sufficient Father

When my twin sons Kevin and Keith were in high school, one of their schoolmates put a gun to his head and shot himself. I was stunned. The boy was only sixteen, the son of a wealthy and respected doctor. I asked Kevin if the boy had been under any unusual pressure.

"No, Dad," he replied. "I saw him just three hours before it happened."

"Did he show any signs of unusual stress?" I asked.

"No, but about an hour after he got home from school he called some of the guys and told them he was going to kill himself."

"What did they do? What did they say to him?" I was intent on discovering why a young man who was active in school, owned horses, went on wonderful vacations, and seemed to have great opportunities would kill himself.

"The guys didn't believe him," Kevin explained. "He hadn't seemed upset, so they thought he was joking."

Only a few days prior to this young man's death, our local newspaper ran the following story about a well-known clinical psychologist:

> The founder of the Psychology Center and a former member of the Community College Board took his life Sunday afternoon, apparently in despair about his health and that of his wife.

"Tonight, I feel tired, alone, and suddenly very old," the psychologist wrote in a note left to his office staff. "The full understanding of these feelings will come only when you too are tired, alone, and old."

A passion for his work also appeared in the note. "During the past thirty-five years, I have done my best to bring understanding and acceptance into the therapeutic relationship with my patients. Rarely does a therapist receive understanding and acceptance in return. Of course, every therapist knows that he should never expect appreciation, and when it does come, it is beautiful and awesome."

The French philosopher Jean-Paul Sartre once wrote, "Things are entirely what they appear to be and behind them there is nothing." Today, thousands of people feel just like Sartre, just like the psychologist, just like my son's schoolmate. Although they seem to have few problems, they're convinced nothing lies beyond life's superficial appearances. Overwhelmed and broken by a void of nothingness, some kill themselves or become addicted to drugs they hope will "free" them from the emptiness they feel. Anything seems better, or more significant, than life as it is.

No matter how great our earthly resources may be—friends, family, wealth, security, recognition—they are not an invincible fortress against the pressures of life. The external pressures over which we have little control—losing a job, financial disaster, personal tragedy, or serious family problems—can become too much for us.

Some of us suffer from inner despair: the unexplainable yet dreadful feeling of emptiness, loneliness, and fear that the Germans call *Angst*. We run from one adviser to another, seeking release from our inner turmoil.

Others suffer from the sheer boredom of daily routines. We rebel against doing the same unbearably mundane tasks over and over again. Suddenly we can't stand to go to the office, talk with friends on the phone, make another cup of coffee, or drive the kids to one more activity.

Today we see a growing number of people whose resources are insufficient to sustain them through the trials of life. But help does exist. God can meet the deepest needs of our lives, even when we face external pressures, inner despair, or excruciatingly dull daily routines. In 2 Corinthians

1, Paul speaks of a God who is sufficient to meet all the pressures we face in life, One who is faithful to carry His children through them. Our all-sufficient Father can comfort and sustain us through life's pressures and enable us to live as victorious Christians!

As we study the first chapter of 2 Corinthians, we will come to know God as the all-sufficient Father—the God of all comfort, the God who raises the dead, the God of all grace, and the God who is faithful.

CHAPTER 1

The God
of All Comfort

S everal years ago a submarine, with all its crew, sank off the Atlantic coast of North America. Once the vessel was located, frogmen went down to assess the damage and the possibility of salvaging the wreck.

As the divers neared the hull of the vessel, they were surprised to hear a message being pounded in Morse code. Someone actually was alive in the submarine! The divers listened carefully. The message was a frantic question beat against the walls of the aquatic tomb: "Is there hope? Is there hope?"

You and I may pose the same question when a problem or tragedy strikes us. Who, after all, is totally free from the crushing pain of losing a loved one, the burden of ill health, the fear of financial difficulties, the anguish of a fragmented home, or any of a hundred other problems?

When such problems beset us, we may feel trapped and submerged by the weight of our circumstances. We wonder, *Is there any hope of overcoming this problem? Can anyone really comfort us in our pain?* We embark on a desperate search for comfort—but usually wind up unfulfilled.

WE HAVE A SOURCE OF COMFORT

As Christians, we have a God who delights in comforting people's hearts. He is our answer to harassment from external pressures. Look what

Paul says about the God of comfort:

> Praise be to the God and Father of our Lord Jesus Christ, the Father of compassion and the God of all comfort, who comforts us in all our troubles, so that we can comfort those in any trouble with the comfort we ourselves have received from God. For just as the sufferings of Christ flow over into our lives, so also through Christ our comfort overflows. If we are distressed, it is for your comfort and salvation; if we are comforted, if is for your comfort, which produces in you patient endurance of the same sufferings we suffer. And our hope for you is firm, because we know that just as you share in our sufferings, so also you share in our comfort (2 Cor. 1:3–7).

In this passage, it is not just Paul who describes aspects of God's character. The apostle says God Himself declares that He is the Father of compassion and the God of all comfort. In fact, Paul uses a derivative of the word *comfort* ten times in these verses. So when we face external pressures—as all of us do from time to time—we can be assured that we have a Heavenly Father who is the Father of compassion and comfort.

Another Bible version uses the term "the Father of mercies" (2 Cor. 1:3, RSV): He is able to forgive us and receive us when other people won't. When we've really blown it and feel that no one wants to have anything to do with us, we have a Father whose arms are open wide. He says, "My son, my daughter, come to Me. I love you even though you've blown it. I know exactly what you've done. I am the Father of mercy. I will show you mercy, even if others won't." We may have guilt on our conscience that we dare not share with anyone. But God knows all about it, and the blood of Jesus Christ cleanses us from our sin. God says, "Listen, I am waiting for you. I am willing to cleanse you and make you a brand-new person. I am the Father of mercy. I understand the trouble you're in." He says He is the God of all comfort. What a wonderful title! What a wonderful God we worship!

However, to embrace God's compassion and comfort, we first must acknowledge that we have troubles. One of the worst mistakes we can make is to pretend nothing's wrong—to hide our emotions and act "cool" or "in control." We put on a mask to disguise our true feelings. But it's a phony

THE GOD OF ALL COMFORT

front that only adds to our despair and anxiety. By keeping our emotions stuffed in our pockets we simply aggravate our inner turmoil.

It's not uncommon to approach an acquaintance and say, "How are you doing, Joe?" Joe says he's just fine, doing great. But a few days later we learn that his wife recently left him for another man. And we think, *But I just saw Joe the other day and he said everything was fine. He seemed so sincere.*

In spite of his efforts to disguise the truth, Joe surely was experiencing a tremendous amount of suffering. Who can comfort a person when his partner—who promised lifelong fidelity—has found another love? The God of all comfort, that's who.

I knew of a boy in the San Francisco area whose father, an ungodly man, drank heavily and was unfaithful to his wife. Several years ago the father died. Today the boy is a wonderful young man who is following the Lord. But inside, he hurts. One day he talked with his mother and said, "Mom, I'm so glad I'm committed to Christ and am happy in Him. I just wish I had a father." Who can comfort that boy in his situation? The God of all comfort, that's who.

You may think your situation is special and you're beyond God's comfort. But God is the God of *all* comfort. No case is too difficult for Him. "I am the LORD, the God of all mankind," God says. "Is anything too hard for me?" (Jer. 32:27).

Paul repeatedly emphasizes the fact that God is completely adequate to comfort us under any circumstance. When Paul wrote to the Philippians, he claimed that "My God will meet all your needs according to his glorious riches in Christ Jesus" (4:19). He is our ultimate source of encouragement and consolation in all of life's circumstances.

GOD COMFORTS US IN THE MIDST OF OUR TROUBLES

Paul knew from firsthand experience what suffering was about. But he also knew what it meant to receive comfort from his Heavenly Father. He describes God as someone "who comforts us in all our troubles, so that we can comfort those in any trouble with the comfort we ourselves have received from God" (2 Cor. 1:4). Notice that God doesn't always deliver us *from* our troubles, but comforts us *in* our troubles. While we're going through afflictions and external harassment, the Father of mercy and the God of all comfort comforts us.

My partner evangelist Dan Owens tells of a time when one of his sons, just five years old at the time, came running across the backyard and fell face first onto the deck. When the screaming and the bleeding finally stopped, and the doctor phoned back to assure Dan and his wife that little Ben would be fine, Dan sat down in his recliner with his son, holding an ice pack against Ben's lips.

Once the crying subsided, so did Dan's parental fears. So after about thirty minutes had passed, Dan asked, "Would you like to get down now?" Ben assured his dad that he did not! Another fifteen minutes passed, and Dan again asked if Ben would like to get down and play. Again, Ben declined. An hour passed, and Ben was quite comfortable right where he was. Finally, after an hour and twenty minutes of sitting on his daddy's lap, that little guy was finally ready to get down and play.

Dan realized that, since Ben had left babyhood, the longest he'd held his son on his lap had been fifteen minutes. But that day, when his son was in such great pain, he held him for an hour and twenty minutes! Why? First, because his son was hurt—and Dan wanted to comfort him. But second, Ben knew his dad wouldn't make him get down so he could move on to something else. Sitting there on his dad's lap, little Ben knew his dad loved him and Ben wanted to soak up all that love and comfort for as long as he could!

Dan remembers thinking of his own times of pain—and I'm sure you can, too. Times when we can almost feel the arms of our Father as we sit on His lap. The Father's comforting voice asks, "Well, do you want to get down now?" And we might respond, "Not yet, Lord, I still hurt." And our Father of compassion is not going to push us away.

How wonderful that we have a Father who scoops us up to comfort us in our suffering! The comfort that little Ben received from his dad was the kind of comfort that Paul received from his Heavenly Father. And we receive it too.

You see, Paul needed a lot of comfort. From the day he was converted, Paul faced all sorts of suffering and trouble. Just a few days after his conversion, he went to the synagogue and began proclaiming Jesus as the Messiah. What happened? People tried to kill him. In fact, Paul was persecuted severely throughout his life. He was stoned. He was thrown in jail. He was shipwrecked. He was criticized. He went through more troubles, attacks, and insults than any of us will ever go through. Yet he became a great man of God.

In a day and age when comfortable Christianity is becoming increasingly popular, we must remember that we *will* share abundantly in Christ's sufferings. Too often, we buy into the idea that if we're walking in the Spirit, we will lead trouble-free lives. Then, when trouble confronts us, we start to cry out, "Why does God allow these things to happen to me? I'm not a bad person!"

Just because we're going through troubles doesn't mean we've lost God's love or favor. It doesn't mean we aren't walking in the Spirit. It doesn't mean God has left us. What it *does* mean is that we are living in a fallen world. As such, we will experience suffering. But God can comfort us even in the midst of this suffering.

Paul had every reason to feel that his world was falling apart. He had every reason to feel "tired, alone, and old." But he realized that the work he had begun in Corinth was of God, and he had a sure hope that it would be brought to completion. Paul never said we wouldn't experience disappointments, suffering, or problems. But he did say that in Christ there's mercy and comfort in every situation.

Suffering and Sharing

Suffering also has a creative purpose. Paul explains that God can comfort us through other people and, in turn, use us to comfort them (2 Cor. 1:5). In fact, the body of Christ, the church, is a fabulous source of comfort. You may think you don't need your local church, that it doesn't have much to offer. But someday you will need that local group of believers.

My dad died when I was ten years old. All through my teenage years, and even into college, I desperately wanted a father. But no man ever took me under his wing. No man ever served as my surrogate father. No man ever said, "Listen, buddy, you don't have a dad, but I'll be your friend. If you've got questions, talk to me." It wasn't until a member of God's body—an Overseas Crusades missionary named Keith Bentson—reached out to me that someone filled this role.

By then, I was twenty-three.

For thirteen years I had longed for a father. And the only comfort I received during those years was my mother telling me over and over again, "God is your Father. He can comfort you." Yes, God comforted me— but I still wanted a real, living, flesh-and-blood father through whom God could speak. God is the God of all comfort. But notice: He comforts us through other people. He comforted me through Keith.

When a person who's experienced difficult times comforts you, it's a wonderful feeling. Nothing is comparable to having someone say to you, "Hey, listen. I went through the same thing you're facing. May I tell you what God did for me?" That's power! That makes Bible verses come alive. That makes God's promises real to the one who is suffering, because another person has gone through it. It can even help the comforter realize why he or she went through a difficult experience. So don't file away the trouble you've gone through. Remember to share it when you see someone else in trouble.

Many years ago my wife, Pat, came face-to-face with cancer. Since then, God has used her to counsel and encourage other people who are facing great troubles. Having gone through the agony of a serious illness, she understands what pain is. She understands what it is like to go to a hospital, to be left alone with a bunch of flowers and a nurse who says "Good morning, everybody!" She understands those who are hurting and can comfort them.

No one, though, seems to be able to comfort people as an older Christian can. When I get in trouble or am in pain, I go to the older people in my church and to my mature Christian friends. During those first few difficult days after Pat and I learned she had cancer, our personal "fathers of the faith" were a great encouragement to us. We often talked with Ray Stedman, a pastor who was instrumental in my coming to the United States; Dick Hillis, founder of OC International; and Albert J. Wollen, our pastor. From these believers, we received wise counsel and comfort.

Older Christians, therefore, should be excited! They have a ministry that young people rarely possess. They can comfort others through their experiences. They have gone through life's troubles and can offer the encouragement that "this too shall pass."

Are you the kind of Christian others turn to for counsel? Do they know you have met the God of all comfort? Have you realized, as Paul did, that no matter how severe the pressures of life become, they never can separate us from the tenderness and compassion of our Heavenly Father?

At a Bible conference I met a family who I believe illustrates what the Apostle Paul wanted the Corinthians to grasp in these opening verses of 2 Corinthians. This family obviously had met the Father of mercy and God of all comfort.

Of the four children in the family, the oldest is a beautiful young woman in perfect health. But all three of her brothers suffer serious handicaps. Two have a dwarf condition and must use crutches to get around. In addition, they suffer from numerous physical complications that have necessitated countless surgeries.

Despite the physical suffering these boys have gone through, and the anguish their parents and sister have felt, they are at peace.

One night at the fireside during the Bible conference, each of the boys spoke about his personal relationship with Jesus Christ. Afterward, the whole family sang a song by Bill and Gloria Gaither that says, "You're something special, you're the only one of your kind." Thinking of them singing that song still brings tears to my eyes. Their testimony revolutionized my view of suffering. What a way to look at life from God's perspective! This is what Paul is talking about.

Because of what this family has been through, and their ability to view their circumstances from God's perspective, they have been an encouragement to hundreds of others. People travel miles just to be with them. They have known the God of all comfort and have become a blessing to others.

No matter how great our burdens or how deep our pain, God is able to comfort us. No matter how severe the pressures of daily life, they can't separate us from the tenderness and compassion of our Heavenly Father. When we allow God to comfort us, His power and grace are magnified. Then God can equip us to comfort others and introduce them to our all-sufficient Father.

As we experience life's troubles and learn to walk with the unfailing Father of mercy and God of all comfort, we can become a source of blessing to others. When we meet the living God and experience His mercy and comfort, we can pass on the reality of the living Christ. All we need to do is believe He is who He says He is. We simply must allow Him to step into our special situations and fill us with His mercy and comfort. He has done it for many others; He will do it for you!

FOR PERSONAL REFLECTION

Read 2 Corinthians 1:3–7.

1. "Who, after all, is totally free from the crushing pain of losing a loved one, the burden of ill health, the fear of financial difficulties, the anguish of a fragmented home, or any of a hundred other problems?" When was a time in your life when you experienced exceptional pain or troubles? Did you ever wonder, "Is there hope?"

2. "Paul knew from firsthand experience what suffering was about. But he also knew what it meant to receive comfort from his Heavenly Father." How does God comfort you as your Heavenly Father? How does His comfort compare or contrast with the comfort (or lack thereof) you received from your earthly father?

3. "Notice that God doesn't always deliver us *from* our troubles, but comforts us *in* our troubles." According to 2 Corinthians 1:3–7, what are some purposes God may be trying to bring about by comforting you instead of delivering you in your current situation?

4. "God can comfort us through other people, and in turn, use us to comfort them." How do you best receive comfort from others?

5. "Despite the physical suffering these boys have gone through, and the anguish their parents and sister have felt, they are at peace." Do you really believe God's comfort can help you and give you peace? In a similar situation, could you be satisfied with God's comfort and peace instead of receiving physical healing?

FOR INTERACTIVE DISCUSSION

Read aloud 2 Corinthians 1:3–7.

1. In 2 Corinthians 1:3–7, Paul is describing aspects of God's character. What do these verses tell us about God's character?

2. "To embrace God's compassion and comfort, we first must acknowledge that we have troubles." Why is it often difficult for us to acknowledge (to ourselves and to others) that we have troubles? What else keeps us from embracing God's compassionate comfort?

3. "While we're going through troubles and external harassment, the Father of mercy and the God of all comfort comforts us." Why does God choose to comfort us in our troubles instead of delivering us from them?

4. "God is the God of all comfort. But notice: He comforts us through other people." Describe a time when God used others to comfort you. Describe a time when you were able to comfort others out of your own experience.

5. "Are you the kind of Christian others turn to for counsel? Do they know you have met the God of all comfort?" What characteristics do you expect to find in a person to whom you turn for counsel and comfort? What process does God use to make us people who can comfort and minister to others? What could you do to better minister comfort to others?

CHAPTER 2

The God Who Raises the Dead

Aphilosopher once commented: "God is dead. Marx is dead. And I don't feel so good myself." This remark is far from humorous. In fact, I believe it reflects the inner pessimism and despair that many people currently feel toward life.

Despair seems to have several different forms. The most common type occurs when a person is beset by "external" troubles—such as financial difficulties or poor health. People who experience this particular form of despair usually are convinced that if only their external circumstances were better, they'd feel fine.

On the other hand, some people experience inner despair even though their external circumstances are ideal. They have all the money they want, all the friends they need, all the education they can stand—but an inexplicable emptiness still haunts them. This type of despair may well be the worst; its source is not definable and it's suffered alone.

We often consider Paul to be the dynamic, unquenchable apostle, but he too suffered from inner despair. Paul's despair, however, was not due to "external" failures or the emptiness that accompanies the quest for personal gain. Rather, his resulted from difficult circumstances he faced in the fulfillment of his ministry. Yet Paul found comfort and victory in the God who raises the dead—a comfort we can find too! Look closely at what he says:

> We do not want you to be uninformed, brothers, about the
> hardships we suffered in the province of Asia. We were under great pres-
> sure, far beyond our ability to endure, so that we despaired even of life.
> Indeed, in our hearts we felt the sentence of death. But this happened
> that we might not rely on ourselves, but on God, who raises the
> dead. He has delivered us from such a deadly peril, and he will deliv-
> er us. On him we have set our hope that he will continue to deliver
> us, as you help us by your prayers. Then many will give thanks on our
> behalf for the gracious favor granted us in answer to the prayers of many
> (2 Cor. 1:8–11).

You may think these verses deal only with the future physical resurrection, when Christ comes again and the dead in Christ will rise, be transformed, and forever be with our Lord. But when Paul speaks of the God
who raises the dead, he means much more than the resurrection of the body
described in Revelation 20:4–5. He also means the resurrection of the soul
and spirit of the inner man.

Perhaps you've gone through an experience similar to Paul's. Notice
what he writes: "We were under great pressure, far beyond our ability to
endure, so that we despaired even of life" (2 Cor. 1:8). Then he goes on
to say, "Indeed, in our hearts we felt the sentence of death." The sentence
of death! Paul is absolutely demoralized! He is, in effect, exclaiming,
"Friends, I thought I was dead. I was finished. That was the end of me."

Have you ever felt that way? Have you ever been so worn out that you
felt as though you had received the sentence of death? Have you come to
the point spiritually where you've felt, *I've had it. I can't take it anymore.
Everything I've built and planned for is smashed. This is the end of the rope.
I have tried to regain hope. I have prayed. I have agonized. I have gone to coun-
selors and a psychiatrist. I've gone to everybody, but nothing seems to work. I've
had it!*

Believe it or not, that could be the most exciting moment of your life!
At that moment you, as a human being, have come to the end. You have
come to the end of trusting your own ego, your own abilities, your own
wealth, and your own education. All the secure supports you've built up
around yourself have fallen away. Suddenly you're flat on your face. You
cry out, "O God, how could this happen to me?"

This experience happens to each of us because of our stubborn, unbelievably misplaced self-confidence. We are convinced we can live our lives on our own. Then an emergency comes along. All our dreams and plans—everything we've imagined for ourselves—go up in smoke. And we cry out, "O Lord, help me. I'm going down."

And the Lord says, "At last. You're finally where I wanted you. Now I can step in. You've had it? Good! I'm the God of those who have had it. You're through? Great! I'm the God for those who are through."

It's so healthy to reach that point of surrender. Then when we reach that point, we have only one way to go. We finally must say, "God, if You are the God who raises the dead, please raise me up. When You raise me up, please have Your way in my life." That can be the greatest moment in a person's life. That can be a moment of real victory. Christ then can step into the situation that is troubling us. He can take over the haunting inner despair of our hearts that we share with no one. He can cleanse us and transform us. He can fill us with His Spirit and give us peace. That is what Paul means when he writes, "But this happened that we might not rely on ourselves but on God, who raises the dead" (v. 9).

A LESSON FROM MY OWN EXPERIENCE

Before coming to the United States to study at Multnomah Biblical Seminary in Portland, Oregon, I did my best to faithfully serve the Lord in Argentina. I had been baptized, received good Bible teaching, and been involved in an evangelistic ministry. My friends and I had gone door to door and passed out tracts. We had a musical team. We started a radio program. It was so exciting at first. But after a few months I realized no one was being converted. We preached on street corners—few people, if any, stopped to listen. We taught children in Bible classes—they listened, and even brought their parents. But no one received Christ.

We decided that what we needed was more prayer. So every Friday, with the help of coffee and cookies, we would spend all night in prayer. We would confess our sins and lay hands on one another and quote Bible promises. Then we would sing some hymns and pray some more. By the time we left Saturday morning at six o'clock, we felt tremendous power. We were sure that now we were men of God.

And for a few hours, everything went well. Then life happened. In my case, I had five little sisters whom I helped care for since my father had died.

I was only nineteen years old, and my sisters would drive me crazy. I had just spent the night with God and my sisters would start fighting and screaming. I would come exploding out of my room and grab my sisters and shake them. "What are you shouting about? Don't you know I'm praying?"

Suddenly I would feel so awful. I'd think, *What's going on? I've just spent all night in prayer. I want to be a man of God. And because two little girls start shouting at each other, I lose my sanctification in thirty seconds.* I just couldn't understand it.

The next Friday arrived and all of us came crawling back like worms, after we had left the previous Saturday flying like jet planes! We felt like such failures, so we would start praying again and reading more verses and singing more songs. By Saturday morning we were tigers again. We were ready to take on the world.

After a few months of this roller-coaster spiritual experience, some of the guys started dropping out. It just didn't seem to be worth it to stay up all night when it didn't even work. I mean, we'd pray and we'd pray—and before you knew it we were coveting girls or losing our temper or twisting the truth to get our own way. After all this effort, you finally begin to say to yourself, *Either the Gospel doesn't work or I'm so corrupt that it doesn't work on me. Something's wrong.* And yet we knew the power of the Gospel was true. We knew we belonged to Christ, but something was missing.

So by the time I came to Multnomah, I was spiritually exhausted. I had done my best. I had tried so hard, yet I seemed to lack power. I had been taught to read the Bible and to pray, but I never had been taught to rely on God in my daily life. I had the assurance of eternal life, but I didn't know the God who raises the dead. I had no authority. I had no joy. It all had drained out.

That first semester at Multnomah, one of my teachers, Dr. George Kehoe, began every class by reciting Galatians 2:20: "I have been crucified with Christ and I no longer live, but Christ lives in me. The life I live in the body I live by faith in the Son of God, who loved me and gave himself for me." I'm ashamed to say that I began to get irritated at Dr. Kehoe's daily recitation. *Doesn't he know we already know that verse?* I thought. Little did I realize that I most definitely did not know that verse the way Dr. Kehoe lived it.

As the semester progressed, I became increasingly discouraged in my spirit. Nearly all my classes pertained to the Bible, so I was getting my fill of Bible study. Unfortunately, most of this study was getting to my head, not my heart. I continued doing the right spiritual activities—teaching Sunday School, preaching, and even speaking in chapel—but in my soul I was desperate.

Just before Christmas break Major Ian Thomas, founder and general director of the Torchbearers—the group that operates Capernwray Hall Bible School in England and other schools around the world—spoke at a Multnomah chapel service. What do you think Major Thomas' key verse was? Galatians 2:20!

Using Moses and the burning bush as his example, Major Thomas showed how Moses spent the first forty years of his life thinking he was really somebody—he had all the money and power he could want. Then the Lord took Moses out of Egypt, and he spent forty years tending sheep, thinking he was absolutely nobody. Finally, during the last forty years of his life, Moses realized he wasn't important—but God in him was! The big lesson God was trying to teach Moses through the burning bush was that it's not the bush that counts; it's God in the bush. Any old bush will do—as long as God's in the bush.

Major Thomas explained that many Christian workers fail because they think they have something to offer God. He explained how he had thought God could use him because of his aggressive, winsome personality. But God didn't use him until he came to the end of himself. *That's exactly my situation,* I thought. *I am at the end of myself.*

I suddenly began to understand Galatians 2:20. After that chapel service, I ran up to my dorm room, knelt, and said, "Lord, I'm beginning to get it. You are the God who indwells me. You are the God who raises the dead. Now I know how to live the Christian life. I don't live it; You live it in me!

You can't imagine the release I felt as a result of that chapel talk. My years of searching had come to an end. I was beginning to understand that Christ lives within each Christian, enabling him or her to live a life that is pleasing to God.

That day was the intellectual turning point of my spiritual life. I had such peace in knowing that I could stop struggling to live the Christian life on my own; it was almost like being converted all over again! However, it took much longer for me to understand—in practical, day-to-day terms—how the indwelling Christ works in the life of a Christian.

Ray Stedman, with whom I spent my break after that semester, helped me learn those vital, practical lessons. I saw Christ in his life and realized, through his example, that a person could live in Christ.

I shared my spiritual frustrations with Ray. At first, he didn't say much. Then, one day, he put his arm around me and said, "You know, Luis, you are so arrogant and so self-confident and think so much of yourself, that someday you're going to end up in serious trouble. You're going to dig a hole for yourself, bury yourself in it, and you won't even know what happened."

I was surprised. I didn't understand what he was talking about. *Me? Arrogant? Self-confident? Why, I'm just a nice guy.* So I said, "Ray, what do you mean by that?"

"Look," he replied, "you think you've got it all. You think because you've come from Argentina and have a pretty good education you can serve the Lord on your own."

I didn't like what Ray was saying one bit. And I didn't like the way he didn't shout at me. I didn't like the way he hugged me as he spoke. *If you are going to insult me,* I thought, *at least shout about it. Don't speak softly and put a compassionate arm around me.*

When I got back to Multnomah I thought, *This is the end. Ray is right. I don't have what it takes. I don't belong in Bible school. I should forget about preaching. I'm going back to business school.* I felt as though I was finished, that I didn't belong in the ministry, that I'd never be an evangelist, that I should go home and support my mom and sisters.

Just as I was facing that crushing, despairing, "I am dead" experience, I remembered Galatians 2:20. I realized once again that I still was trying to live the Christian life on the basis of my own ability and power. What I needed was to stop relying on myself and rely on God. I needed to stop relying on my own Bible knowledge and rely on God. I needed to stop relying on my prayer life and rely on God.

When I finally *did* begin to rely on God rather than all these other things, my life took on a whole new meaning. It wasn't *me* trying to serve the Lord anymore. It was me relying on *Him!* What a change!

It doesn't matter whether or not we are beautiful, whether or not we are brilliant in theology, whether or not we are loaded with Bible knowledge, whether or not we speak eloquently. All that matters is that we rely on the God who raises the dead—and that Jesus Christ indwells us. That's the lesson Paul had to learn in Asia. He had to be unbearably crushed so that he would learn to rely not on himself, but on the indwelling God who raises the dead.

Today we must learn the same lesson. We must not rely on our own knowledge, our own skill, our dynamic pastor, or the super church to which we belong. We must rely on the indwelling Christ—the God who raises us from the dead. As the Father of compassion, the God of all comfort, and the God who raises the dead, He can fill the void in our lives. He can make us new creatures, alive in the living Christ!

FOR PERSONAL REFLECTION

Read 2 Corinthians 1:8–11.

1. "Have you ever felt so worn out that you felt as though you had received the sentence of death?" What did you do with your feelings of despair? How did God meet you in your despair?

2. "I'm the God of those who have had it. You're through? Great! I'm the God for those who are through." In what areas of your life have you had it? What might God be beckoning you to surrender?

3. "We finally must say, 'God, if You are the God who raises the dead, please raise me up.'" What would it look like for God to "raise the dead" in your life? Right now, ask Him to do just that.

4. "Any old bush will do—as long as God's in the bush" (Major Ian Thomas). How does God's presence in you make a difference in your daily life?

FOR INTERACTIVE DISCUSSION

Read aloud 2 Corinthians 1:8–11.

1. "We were under great pressure, far beyond our ability to endure, so that we despaired even of life" (1 Cor. 1:8b). What kind of hardships and despair did Paul and his companions experience? Why did Paul say that these incredible hardships had happened?

2. "At that moment you, as a human being, have come to the end." What brings a person to this place? Why could the experience of "coming to the end" of yourself be the most exciting moment of your life? *What might be the dangerous option at this crisis point?*

3. "I was spiritually exhausted. I had done my best. I had tried so hard, yet I seemed to lack power." Why does expending great effort not automatically produce great spiritual power and growth? Perhaps God has brought you through a similar experience. Share your story with the group.

4. "What I needed was to stop relying on myself and rely on God." What is the key to experiencing authentic spiritual power? What would this look like in your life?

CHAPTER 3

The God of Grace

The God we worship is the God of mercy and comfort who raises the dead. That much we've already discussed. Yet in the first chapter of 2 Corinthians, Paul also refers to Him as the God of all grace. That means He is the God who produces character in us—who molds our character through our life experiences, even the bothersome little problems of life.

I'm the kind of person who likes big problems. They're a challenge to me. Give me a seemingly impossible task—like winning a nation for Christ—and I love it. Tell me that the leader of a given country is resisting our efforts to preach the Gospel among his people, and I'll gladly devote weeks to finding a solution to this dilemma. But bother me with a stupid, little problem—like a door that sticks or a microphone that won't work—and I go crazy.

Often it's the little problems, not the big ones, that reveal the real weaknesses in our character. But the God of grace is with us and in us, enabling us to handle all the problems we encounter in daily life. God wants to take over the regular, dull, humdrum, daily affairs of our lives, and reproduce His holiness, sincerity, and wisdom in us.

THE GOD OF GRACE WANTS US TO LIVE FULL LIVES

In my ministry, I have counseled many people who are bored with certain aspects of their lives—their jobs, their spouses, their vacations, their friends, their homes. Often these people appear to have great jobs, perfect families, active social lives, and nice homes. Yet inside, they are so bored they can hardly stand it.

I, too, have experienced boredom in my life. One of the most boring periods of my life occurred when I worked for the Bank of London in Argentina. Partly because I spoke both English and Spanish, I had tremendous opportunities for advancement. Yet, in spite of what appeared to be a great job, I was bored stiff with the routine.

How can people be bored when their lives seem to be going great? Is there a solution to the problem of boredom? I think Dr. Harold Dodds understands this problem very well when he says: "It is not the fast tempo of modern life that kills, but the boredom, a lack of strong interest, and failure to grow that destroy. It is the feeling that nothing is worthwhile that makes men ill and unhappy."

How true! When we think our lives are not worthwhile, we become bored. Life becomes almost unbearable. But this is not how the God of grace intends us to live! Jesus said, "I have come that they may have life, and have it to the full" (John 10:10). God doesn't want us to live life halfheartedly. He has exciting plans for us! He wants us to live life to the fullest. That is a part of His grace.

I would be willing to venture that the Apostle Paul was never bored with his life. Paul knew that his ultimate purpose was to please God, and he pursued that goal with all his might. So he writes, "I press on toward the goal to win the prize for which God has called me heavenward in Christ Jesus" (Phil. 3:14).

When we seek to please God and walk according to His will, we will not be bored. We will live full lives. We can take God's promise to heart: "'For I know the plans I have for you,' declares the LORD, 'plans to prosper you and not to harm you, plans to give you hope and a future'" (Jer. 29:11).

THE GOD OF GRACE ENABLES US TO LIVE WITH A CLEAR CONSCIENCE

When the God of grace is in control of every area of our lives—big or small, exciting or ordinary—we also can boast in our conscience. Read what Paul writes about this:

Now this is our boast: Our conscience testifies that we have
conducted ourselves in the world, and especially in our relations with
you, in the holiness and sincerity that are from God. We have done
so not according to worldly wisdom but according to God's grace. For
we do not write you anything you cannot read or understand. And I
hope that, as you have understood us in part, you will come to understand fully that you can boast of us just as we will boast of you in the
day of the Lord Jesus (2 Cor. 1:12–14).

Can you imagine standing up and saying, "You know, I can boast
because my conscience accuses me of nothing!" Yet that's exactly what Paul
is saying. He boldly proclaims that he has a conscience that can boast. He
can look other people directly in the eye and say, "Hey, I have nothing to
hide. My sins have been washed away. Though I'm a sinner, I've been made
right before God. Nothing is between me and Him." He even continues,
"I'm free. I've cleared my conscience with other people. I don't need to wear
a mask."

Many of us would give anything to be able to say what Paul is saying.
We would give anything to live with a clear conscience. But many of us
never realize that all we have to do is make a simple confession of faith.
Before God, we must admit that we have sinned and—through the blood
of Jesus Christ—need His forgiveness. Once that's done, God will clear
out all the skeletons locked away in our closets. God will help everyone
who comes to Him. He will help us go to the people we have offended and
clear up the problems that have plagued our conscience for years.

When I was in middle school in Argentina, I stole a box of colored
pencils that belonged to a boy named John Payne. Stealing those pencils
didn't bother me at first. Later, though, when I straightened out my life
and began walking closer with the Lord, my conscience wouldn't let me
forget that incident. *Luis,* I would think, *when are you going to pay back
John for the pencils you stole?* Then I would answer, *Be serious, Luis, you don't
even know where John Payne is anymore!*

But the Lord never let me forget that incident. It bothered my conscience. And though I knew that the box of pencils wasn't all that important to John Payne, it was vital to me that I clear my conscience before God.
I even remember praying one day, "Lord, if I ever run into John again, I'll

give him ten boxes of pencils! Please remove this guilt and restore my fellowship with You."

Years later, I came to the United States. Ray Stedman asked if I could preach at a church in the San Francisco Bay area. I told him I'd be happy to. He then asked, "Can you have dinner with one of the elders prior to the meeting?"

"Sure," I replied. "What's his name?"

"John Payne."

No! I thought. *It couldn't be the same John Payne whose pencils I stole in Argentina! If it is, this would be a wonderful opportunity to finally clear my conscience of this problem.*

When I arrived at the house for dinner, it was the same John Payne. As we reminisced, I finally said, "John, this is very embarrassing for me, but when we were in school in Argentina, I stole a box of pencils from you. Will you forgive me and let me pay you back?"

"Forget it, Luis," he replied.

"No, John," I shot back. "I insist that you let me pay you back."

"Luis," he said, "it's forgotten. I'm a grown man. What would I do with a box of colored pencils? I forgive you. Forget about it."

That was exactly what I needed to hear. It felt so good to be free from that burden on my conscience.

It may seem silly to have worried about a box of pencils, but an important lesson is involved here. Many people who sin greatly begin doing so because of unresolved guilt in their lives. Sometimes something as small as stealing a box of pencils or approving small discrepancies in our financial affairs can touch off a tragic chain of events. When we live with unresolved guilt, our conscience eventually becomes hardened and we proceed to more serious things.

This is especially true in the area of sexual relations. It's easy to convince ourselves that just a little flirting is all right, just a few tantalizing thoughts won't do any harm. Surely, flipping channels in a hotel room or checking out an Internet porn site won't hurt anyone. However, by rationalizing immoral behavior or thoughts, we become insensitive to sin. We lose the fear of the Lord. Christians often quote Scripture that says "the fear of the LORD is the beginning of wisdom" (Prov. 1:7, KJV). What's the less frequently recited converse to that proverb? Failure to fear the Lord is the beginning of vice, lust, immorality, and corruption.

My wife told me about a white-haired, seventy-year-old gentleman who went forward when the invitation was given at a camp meeting. People who knew this Christian man couldn't imagine why he went forward. He had been active in the church for many years, and was considered a venerable old saint. "Brother," the minister said, "you've walked with the Lord for most of your life. Why did you come forward tonight?"

"Everyone thinks I'm a great Christian man," he replied, "but I have a problem that has haunted me since I was a boy. I've never been able to deal with it. Tonight, I want to take care of it."

The minister thought, *What problem could this gentleman have?*

The old man continued, "Ever since I was a boy, I've lusted after and coveted women. When I'm alone, I read dirty books and look at pornographic magazines. Tonight I want to clear my conscience before God and rededicate my life to Him."

Can you imagine the guilt this man carried on his conscience for all those years? Please, let's not wait until we're seventy to clear up problems that keep us from enjoying all the blessings the Lord has for us. Let's get down on our knees right now and clear up anything that's preventing us from being free. If we want to have a clear conscience like Paul, a conscience about which we can boast, we must settle things with God and live holy lives before Him.

THE GOD OF GRACE ENABLES US TO LIVE IN HOLINESS

The Apostle Paul further explains the ingredients of a clear conscience in verse 12: "Our conscience testifies that we have conducted ourselves in the world . . . in the holiness and sincerity that are from God. We have done so not according to worldly wisdom but according to God's grace." We can have a clear conscience when we live in holiness and godly sincerity. And we live this way by the grace of God, not by our own wisdom.

In our own power and wisdom, it's impossible for us to understand and live out the concept of holiness. Yet God is holy and demands that His people be holy too. We are to "Make every effort to live in peace with all men and to be holy; without holiness no one will see the Lord" (Heb. 12:14).

In the midst of the world's degenerate moral condition, it's tough for Christians to live in holiness. Those who live in holiness are truly set apart from the world. But if we are to have a conscience about which we can boast, we must live in holiness.

I fear, though, that we are becoming too lax in our pursuit of holiness. We are beginning to play games with God. We are allowing unholiness to exist among us. By our complacency and tolerance, we sanction unholy living. In the name of "nonjudgmentalism" we tolerate activity that God will not tolerate. When a Christian leader falls into immorality, we no longer are shocked. For a fleeting moment we wonder how such a thing could happen, but then forget about it.

God, however, does not forget. He will not tolerate sin. As Paul notes, "Do not be deceived: God cannot be mocked. A man reaps what he sows" (Gal. 6:7). When we commit immorality or other unholy actions, we dishonor God and will reap the penalty of our sin. Even when we repent, we live with consequences of our sin. When we stubbornly continue in our sin, we devastate our own lives and that of others. But when we walk in holiness, transparent before the Lord, our lives will reflect His power and authority.

Living in holiness is not impossible. Jesus' death and resurrection paid the penalty for our sins, making holy living possible. The Holy Spirit, living within us, gives us the power to follow Christ's example of holy living so that we can have fellowship with a holy God. This is why Paul can speak of living with a clear conscience.

The wonderful news is that we can begin holy living at any moment. The blood of Jesus Christ truly cleanses us from all sin and restores our relationship with God.

I have a friend who was divorced from his first wife with whom he had three children. He had walked away, married another woman, and had two more children with his second wife. After a few years and under the conviction of the Holy Spirit, he became distressed by what he had done. The guilt of his unholy actions weighed on him terribly. He had children by both wives and his first wife despised him.

One day he said to me, "Luis, I want to be reconciled to my first wife, but she hates me." Then he said these telling words: "If I had treated my first wife the way I treat my second wife, I never would have divorced."

I told him, "You go and tell your first wife that and maybe she will forgive you."

My friend went to his first wife in humble repentance and she did forgive him, and he was reconciled to her and to his children. They don't live together, of course, because he is married to his second wife, but now his children get along. More importantly, this man has peace. Even his face has changed. He can live with a clear conscience because he has settled his sin with God and with others. He can go forward and live a holy life from here on out.

WE ARE TO LIVE IN GODLY SINCERITY

Paul also says we are to live in godly sincerity. That means we don't wear masks. We don't try to *act* like fine Christians. We don t build up a "Christian" façade to impress other people. Godly sincerity simply means we are who we are in Jesus Christ. It means we walk in the light of the Lord, no longer putting on a show to deceive others.

Christians have no reason to live behind a mask. Christians are admonished to "walk in the light, as he is in the light" (1 John 1:7). This means we are to walk before God and man with the same transparency— or, as Paul says, sincerity—that Christ showed in His life. And by accepting the grace of God, we can do so.

When we place ourselves under the control of the indwelling Christ, we then are able to boast about our conscience and live in godly sincerity. When our hearts are transparent before God, we suffer no guilt from sin; we can boldly proclaim the message of Jesus Christ. We don't have to put on any kind of spiritual show because the power and authority of the Holy Spirit are at work within us.

It's interesting to note that people who walk with the Lord almost always can spot a "religious showman." No matter how much church terminology the showman knows, or how many long prayers the showman recites, a person walking with the Lord will see through the mask. During a time of crisis, spiritual cosmetics will show themselves for the cheap imitations they are. Godly sincerity, on the other hand, also will show itself for what it is during difficult times.

Notice how Paul responded when he faced a difficult situation (2 Cor. 1:13–14). Apparently, false teachers in Corinth had accused him of not being sincere in his letters. Paul responded that his letters have the same godly sincerity as his conduct. Paul still can boast in his conscience. He can say he has thrown the mask away. He has nothing to hide. He is free in Christ.

Realizing, too, that he is not always completely understood, Paul hopes that "on the day of the Lord Jesus" the Corinthians will be as proud of him as he will be of them. Despite their harsh criticism, Paul reveals his true character and affirms his genuine love and confidence in the Corinthians.

Nothing is more humbling to Paul than the expectation of standing before the Lord Jesus in judgment. On that day, all façades will be exposed. Everyone who has hidden behind a mask will be revealed. But those who know the all-sufficient Father, and are controlled by His grace, can live with a clear conscience and godly sincerity until that day.

FOR PERSONAL REFLECTION

Read 2 Corinthians 1:12–14.

1. "He is the God who produces character in us—who molds our character through our life experiences, even the bothersome little problems of life." What "little problems" are bothering you right now? What weaknesses are they revealing in your character?

2. "He [God] will help us go to the people we have offended and clear up the problems that have plagued our conscience for years." Are there any unconfessed sins bothering your conscience? Take care of them today! (1 John 1:9). Is there any relationship you need to mend? If possible, make plans to do so right away.

3. "We don't build up a 'Christian' façade to impress other people. Godly sincerity simply means we are who we are in Jesus Christ." How would you describe who you are in Jesus Christ? What else does it mean to live in godly sincerity? Why is this possible?

4. "Paul . . . can say he has thrown the mask away. He has nothing to hide. He is free in Christ." What masks need to come off in your life?

FOR INTERACTIVE DISCUSSION

Read aloud 2 Corinthians 1:12–14.

1. "It is the feeling that nothing is worthwhile that makes men ill and unhappy" (Dr. Harold Dodds). How did Paul's knowledge of his ultimate purpose in life allow him to live a full life (see Phil. 2:7–3:14)?

2. "We would give anything to live with a clear conscience." How is it possible to live with a clear conscience? How is it possible to live in holiness? How does this differ from being "perfect"?

3. "During a time of crisis, spiritual cosmetics will show themselves for the cheap imitations they are." Can you tell the difference between a religious fake and a sincerely godly person? Think of someone you know who lives a sincerely godly life. How does his or her life impact you?

4. "On that day, all façades will be exposed." How does thinking about standing before the Lord Jesus help us to live holy and sincere lives? How does it help us deal with accusations against our character?

CHAPTER 4

The God Who Is Faithful

In the first part of 2 Corinthians 1, Paul describes the God of all comfort, the God who raises the dead, and the God of all grace. Toward the end of the first chapter, he describes the God who is faithful. Paul uses an unfortunate situation in his own life to emphasize his integrity and to explain the fullness and certainty of God's faithfulness.

Paul said he would visit the Corinthians after going through Macedonia (1 Cor. 16:5). His original itinerary included visits to three locations. First, he would go from Ephesus to Corinth. He then would leave Corinth to visit Macedonia. Finally, he would return to Corinth where the Corinthians were to provide him with escorts for his journey to Judea.

Paul learned of serious problems in the Corinthian church, however, and, because of his love for them, decided not to visit them "with a whip" (1 Cor. 4:21). He didn't want to come as a disciplinarian. Instead, he desired to give the Corinthians more time to set their church in order and repent for having wandered away from God.

Paul decided, therefore, to go straight to Macedonia. That's when the trouble began. Paul's adversaries in Corinth viewed the change in his itinerary as a golden opportunity to discredit the apostle. So he responded to the criticism aimed at him:

Because I was confident of this, I planned to visit you first so that you might benefit twice. I planned to visit you on my way to Macedonia and to come back to you from Macedonia, and then to have you send me on my way to Judea. When I planned this, did I do it lightly? Or do I make my plans in a worldly manner so that in the same breath I say, "Yes, yes" and "No, no"? But as surely as God is faithful, our message to you is not "Yes" and "No" (2 Cor. 1:15–18).

His enemies' accusations did not surprise Paul. Public figures at that time, as today, were targets of gossip and false rumors. Paul did find it difficult to believe, however, that his enemies could so easily persuade the Corinthian converts to believe that the itinerary change indicated a flaw in his character.

Imagine Paul's dismay when his integrity and ministry suddenly were under fire because of an itinerary change, a change that actually was made out of concern for the Corinthians! As Philip E. Hughes states in his book *Paul's Second Epistle to the Corinthians:*

> Indeed, as they well knew, it was in themselves, not in him that the real cause of the change in plan lay: it was they, not he, who were guilty of inconstancy and fickleness; it was they who, after having responded to him with so clear a yea, had admitted into their fellowship false apostles whose object was to persuade them to say nay to their true apostle. Had they remained steadfast and loyal, the plan as originally conceived would have been carried through. His decision, moreover, had not been governed by selfish motives, but by consideration and affection for them (Wm. B. Eerdman's Publishing, p. 34).

It's unfortunate that some believers today, like some Christians in Paul's day, create problems within the body by allowing false teachers to deceive them. These "false teachers" may be proponents of strange theology or self-appointed leaders seeking more than reasonable control in others' lives. They may simply be people given to suspicion and dissension. Satan is a master at inflating petty incidents into monumental problems that threaten to destroy the unity of the body. As the Apostle Peter pointed out, "Be self-controlled and alert. Your enemy the devil prowls around like a roaring lion looking for someone to devour" (1 Peter 5:8).

I have the privilege of traveling thousands of miles every year to preach the Gospel of our Lord Jesus Christ. On several occasions I've had to change my itinerary, usually because of a problem I cannot control—such as the grounding of an airplane due to weather or mechanical problems. Almost every time, though, Satan finds some way of using the itinerary change to create all sorts of problems and unnecessary confrontations.

This is precisely what happened to Paul (2 Cor. 1:17–18). But Paul lovingly reminds the Corinthians that their accusations suggest they question even Almighty God Himself—the God of all comfort, the God who raises the dead, the God of all grace, and, importantly, the God who is faithful.

WE CAN BELIEVE THE PROMISES OF GOD

Paul goes on to explain that the Corinthians have no reason to doubt his faithfulness or the faithfulness of God. He tells the Corinthians that Jesus is the fulfillment of every promise of God:

> For the Son of God, Jesus Christ, who was preached among you by me and Silas and Timothy, was not "Yes" and "No," but in him it has always been "Yes." For no matter how many promises God has made, they are "Yes" in Christ. And so through him the "Amen" is spoken by us to the glory of God (2 Cor. 1:19–20).

Jesus' death and resurrection are our guarantee that God is faithful, that He hears our prayers, and that all His promises are true. Paul clearly explains this to the Corinthians because if they have any doubts about his integrity as God's messenger, they probably doubt God's message too.

I have a hunch that many Christians today, like the Corinthians, occasionally have trouble believing God's promises. Oh, the promises sound nice. Sometimes they even cheer us up. Yet I think many of us have, at least unconsciously, questioned whether God is faithful to keep His promises. We'll sometimes catch ourselves thinking, *Are the promises of God really true?*

Paul knew that God was faithful to keep His promises. He had leaned on the promises of God many times and found them to be true. In fact, I believe it was his utter confidence in the God who promises to sustain His children that kept Paul going. Though he suffered great hardship in life—ill health, betrayal, persecution, loneliness, beatings, destitution—those problems didn't crush him. Even at the end of his life, Paul could say, "That is why I am suffering as I am. Yet I am not ashamed, because I know whom I have believed, and am convinced that he is able to guard what I have entrusted to him for that day" (2 Tim. 1:12).

When the storms of life seem overwhelming, the God of faithfulness wants us to experience His perfect peace. To ensure His faithfulness to His children, God has gone on record numerous times throughout the Bible to give His people great promises.

Joshua, one of my favorite Old Testament characters, knew from experience that God is faithful. Commissioned by God to lead the Children of Israel into the Promised Land, Joshua, trusting in God's faithfulness, had overcome numerous obstacles and defeated powerful enemies. He could state with confidence, "Not one of all the LORD's good promises to the house of Israel failed; every one was fulfilled" (Josh. 21:45).

More than four hundred years later, Solomon still could proclaim, "Praise be to the LORD, who has given rest to his people Israel just as he promised. Not one word has failed of all the good promises he gave through his servant Moses" (1 Kings 8:56).

None of God's promises ever has failed! The great evangelist D. L. Moody confidently stated, "God never made a promise that was too good to be true." Think about that! No wonder Jesus says not to worry about tomorrow (Matt. 6:25). God did not create us to be self-sufficient. He created us to depend on Him. We don't have to rush around trying to solve all our problems and trials in thirty seconds. We don't have to exhaust all of our human problem-solving options before we turn to God as a last resort. Every trial we face is an opportunity for God to demonstrate His loving faithfulness to us.

British preacher Charles Spurgeon once said, "Do not treat God's promises as if they were curiosities for a museum, but believe them and use them."

Let me suggest, then, several guidelines for using the promises of God.

First, we need to deepen our relationship with the God who is faithful. We often separate ourselves from the promises of God because we don't know Him. We learn about God by reading, studying, memorizing, and obeying His Word. Through Bible study and prayer we become better acquainted with God and strengthen our relationship with Him.

Second, we must be sure we are claiming promises rather than general spiritual teaching, and that the promises we claim are intended for us. Some of God's promises, such as those found in Genesis 46:2–4,

Numbers 14:24, and Deuteronomy 28:1–14, were intended for specific people. We can't claim a promise that belongs to someone else! However, we can claim many of the Old Testament promises that are repeated in the New Testament. For example, God promised Joshua, "I will never leave you or forsake you" (Josh. 1:5), and He then extended that promise to modern-day Christians (Heb. 13:5). We can also rely on God's promises to remain true to His character and attributes—everything He has revealed about Himself.

Third, we need to wait for God to fulfill His promises. Once we ask God to meet our need through His promises, we must give Him time to fulfill those promises through our daily experiences. One of the characteristics of a mature Christian is that he or she steadfastly hopes for God's blessing in the midst of adverse circumstances.

God has been faithful to His people in the past and promises to be faithful in the future. Thus, we have no need to worry. We can rest assured that the God who is faithful will fulfill every promise we claim in the name of Jesus.

THE HOLY SPIRIT IS OUR GUARANTEE

While Paul feels the need to defend his integrity, his true concern is the Corinthians' relationship with Christ. He writes:

> Now it is God who makes both us and you stand firm in Christ.
> He anointed us, set his seal of ownership on us, and put his Spirit in
> our hearts as a deposit, guaranteeing what is to come (2 Cor. 1:21–22).

Paul is reminding the Corinthians that the God who is faithful is the one who has put both him and them together in Christ. The same faithful God also keeps both Paul and the Corinthians established in Christ. They are all in this together because of the faithfulness of God!

In verse 22, Paul discusses what the *King James Version* calls the "earnest" of the Spirit. The Greek word for earnest is *arrabon,* a down payment that guarantees that the full amount will be paid later. When Paul speaks of the Holy Spirit as an *arrabon,* he's telling us that the life we live by the power of the Holy Spirit is the first installment and guarantee of greater blessings to come. This is God's pledge to His children. God's faithfulness comes with a living, live-in guarantee—the Holy Spirit Himself.

With the Holy Spirit residing within us, we can accept His guarantee. God is our all-sufficient Father—the God of all comfort, the God who raises the dead, the God of all grace, and the God who is faithful to us through all the trials of life.

FOR PERSONAL REFLECTION

Read 2 Corinthians 1:15–22.

1. "Imagine Paul's dismay when his integrity and ministry suddenly were under fire because of an itinerary change, a change that was actually made out of concern for the Corinthians!" Have you ever been under attack because of misunderstandings about your motives or plans? How did you respond?

2. "Paul goes on to explain that the Corinthians have no reason to doubt his faithfulness or the faithfulness of God." Does your life reflect God's faithfulness? Ask yourself, "How dependable am I?"

3. "I have a hunch that many Christians today, like the Corinthians, occasionally have trouble believing God's promises." What obstacles do you face in believing God's promises? What promises will you choose to live by today?

4. "The life we live by the power of the Holy Spirit is the first installment and guarantee of greater blessings to come." How does the Holy Spirit guarantee future blessings? Ask yourself, "How is His work evident in my life today?"

FOR INTERACTIVE DISCUSSION

Read aloud 2 Corinthians 1:15–22.

1. "Paul uses an unfortunate situation in his own life to emphasize his integrity and to explain the fullness and certainty of God's faithfulness." What was this unfortunate situation Paul is describing (see also 1 Cor. 4:18–21 and 1 Cor. 16:5–8)? How does Paul use this to highlight both God's faithfulness and his own commitment to the Corinthian believers?

2. "For no matter how many promises God has made, they are 'yes' in Christ." Why can we trust God to be faithful to every promise He makes?

3. "Do not treat God's promises as if they were curiosities for a museum; but believe them and use them" (Charles Spurgeon). How can we "use the promises of God"? Share a time when you saw God's faithfulness to His promises firsthand.

4. "Paul is reminding the Corinthians that the God who is faithful constantly establishes them with Christ." How does the Holy Spirit ensure God's faithfulness to us and also our connection to each other?

PART TWO

The Victorious Christian

During preparation for one of our evangelistic festivals in South America, a poor, shabbily dressed man attended our counselor training course. Although the training is open to all spiritually mature Christians, generally the better educated and socially established lay leaders of local churches attend these classes. This man was also illiterate, so he brought his young nephew to read and write for him.

Although the man attended every class, we didn't expect him to do much counseling. Like many illiterate people, however, he had a fantastic memory and had learned much through the counseling classes.

Following one of the evangelistic meetings, every available counselor was busy except the illiterate man. At that time a doctor walked in, requesting counsel. In Latin America, most doctors are sophisticated and fashionable; this doctor was no exception. Before anyone could stop him, the shabbily dressed man took the doctor into a room for counseling.

When our counseling director learned of this, he was a bit concerned. He didn't know if the illiterate man would be able to communicate effectively with the sophisticated doctor. When the doctor came out of the counseling room, our counseling director asked if he could help him in any way.

"No, thank you," the doctor replied. "This fellow has helped me very much."

The next day the doctor returned with two other doctors. Our counseling director wanted to talk with him, but the doctor refused, asking for counsel with the illiterate man. By the end of the festival, that illiterate man had led four doctors and their wives to Christ! He couldn't read or write, but he lived an authentic Christian life.

So often we look on the outside for signs of victorious Christian living. But the outward appearance doesn't count. Outward appearances reveal little of authentic Christian living. What really counts—what really makes a Christian's life vibrant and real—is the power of the living Christ within.

The Apostle Paul knew this principle well. He lived in victory through the power of the indwelling Christ, enduring some of the most horrible experiences a person could face. He had every reason to be down and out, but he knew the all-sufficient Father and knew the secret of living in authentic victory.

Thus, Paul walked transparently before God, aiming to please Him in all that he did. Paul wanted nothing more than to live a holy life in fellowship with God.

Paul struggled to communicate this truth to the Corinthian Christians. They were his spiritual children. He longed for them to experience the energizing power of the indwelling Christ so that they might live victoriously. But the Corinthians had serious problems and had much to learn. So Paul wrote to them, explaining what God expected of them and how God enabled them to live as triumphant Christians. Paul's message, in 2 Corinthians 1:23–7:1, is equally important to Christians today. It can help us discover how to live a life that is pleasing to God—a life that is both authentic and spiritually vibrant!

CHAPTER 5

Restoration Within the Church

As Christians, we enjoy fellowship with God and live victoriously when we obey His commands. But when we, as individuals or as a church, go against God's commands, the whole church suffers. Thus, the church has a God-given responsibility to discipline its members when they publicly sin. It is our duty to restore them to full fellowship with God.

I realize we rarely discuss the topic of disciplining believers who have fallen into public sin. We would rather discuss how to live the victorious Christian life, or similar cheery subjects. But we cannot continue to grow in spiritual maturity until we first understand and obey what God says about this crucial issue.

I often heard Ray Stedman remark, "Woe to the man who has to learn principles at a time of crisis." As much as we'd like to ignore the subject, it's important that we learn the principles of biblical discipline *before* crises develop. The more we learn about what God teaches on this subject, the happier and better equipped we will be to handle crises in our personal, family, and church lives.

God wants us to live happy, joyful Christian lives. God's plan is that every believer, even in the midst of trials and problems, should rest in Him and be content. Every Christian man, woman, and young person who walks in the fullness of the Holy Spirit should be joyous in Jesus Christ. But sin kills joy, and the joy of the Spirit can be regained only when that person is restored to fellowship with God.

All of us commit sin, but our loving God has provided a way for us to be cleansed. In addition to confessing our sin to God and receiving His forgiveness, cleansing from public sin comes through church discipline, which Paul carefully explains in 2 Corinthians 1:23–2:13. This passage deals with the difficult subject of sin and discipline within the local church, and presents it in the context of restoration and rejoicing.

DISOBEDIENCE BRINGS UNHAPPINESS TO THE CORINTHIAN CHURCH

When Paul first went to Corinth, he confronted a wild city—perhaps the Las Vegas of its day. But during the eighteen months Paul preached the Gospel in Corinth, many men and women—Jews, Gentiles, commoners, as well as upper-class people—came to Christ, and a strong church was established.

The church in Corinth was greatly blessed; its members had tremendous spiritual gifts. In fact, it seems that all the gifts of the Spirit were evident there. Because of their spiritual gifts, however, the Corinthian Christians thought they were better than Christians in other churches. In their pride and self-satisfaction, they became dangerously weak.

Before long, the Corinthians had a serious problem—a problem they didn't even recognize. Yet Paul was aware of it and knew its cause. In his first letter to the Corinthians, Paul exposed their problem and told them exactly what to do about it. "It is actually reported that there is sexual immorality among you," Paul writes, "and of a kind that does not occur even among pagans: A man has his father's wife. And you are proud! Shouldn't you rather have been filled with grief and have put out of your fellowship the man who did this?" (1 Cor. 5:1–2).

As shocking as this act of immorality was, the Corinthians' complacent attitude toward the sinners distressed Paul even more. Rather than being grieved by the sin, they looked the other way, even though God explicitly forbade the sin (Lev. 18:8). Because some of their members were rich in spiritual gifts, they had become proud and pretended not to notice their weakness. Paul rebuked them, insisting that they discipline the offender so he could not pervert the purity of the church.

After receiving Paul's letter, the Corinthians were crushed. They lost their joy. And that was the result Paul expected. He tells the Corinthians they were disheartened because they had been disobedient to God (2 Cor. 7:9).

Paul knew a direct connection exists between disobedience to God and a lack of joy and excitement in a Christian's life. When we live in obedience to God, we experience freedom, happiness, excitement, and love. But if we can't pray with David, "You anoint my head with oil; my cup overflows" (Ps. 23:5), something is wrong with our obedience. We can't blame our in-laws, our uncles, our spouses, or our jobs. Being out of step with God depresses a person. And when a church steps away from biblical truth, a curtain of darkness covers the congregation.

Paul's letter caused such severe turmoil that he visited the Corinthians a second time. In the process, his enemies stirred up more gossip, which nearly broke his heart. After he left, and through many tears, Paul wrote the Corinthians another letter of rebuke (a letter now lost) that was more severe. Because of the Corinthians' bitterness, sorrow, and lack of joy, Paul refused to visit them until they took the proper steps to restore their joy.

He explains his actions regarding the disobedience of the church at Corinth:

> I call God as my witness that it was in order to spare you that I did not return to Corinth. Not that we lord it over your faith, but we work with you for your joy, because it is by faith you stand firm. So I made up my mind that I would not make another painful visit to you. For if I grieve you, who is left to make me glad but you whom I have grieved? I wrote as I did so that when I came I should not be distressed by those who ought to make me rejoice. I had confidence in all of you, that you would all share my joy. For I wrote you out of great distress and anguish of heart and with many tears, not to grieve you but to let you know the depth of my love for you (2 Cor. 1:23–2:4).

As a result of the Corinthians' despondency, Paul changed his travel plans. Instead of visiting the Corinthians while they were so unhappy, Paul sent Titus to help resolve the problem. Paul wanted to give the Corinthians time to regain their joy before he came to them. He wanted to see the love between members, the joy in worship, and the praise of God that fills an obedient congregation.

DISCIPLINE IS NECESSARY

The Corinthian church finally recognized its disobedience and obeyed Paul's admonition. The Corinthians disciplined their disobedient member. They called him into the assembly and told him what Paul had said. They took away the privilege of the Lord's Supper and separated him from the assembly (2:6). The biblical record shows that this individual was humbled and broken by the action taken against him.

After reviewing the complex situation of the Corinthian church, and the great pain, sorrow, and suffering Paul's firm rebuke caused, you may think the apostle's instructions were cruel and harsh. That's not the case. The church took strong action to make the man aware of his immorality so he could repent and be restored to fellowship.

What do you think your church would have done in this situation? Unfortunately, few churches today will discipline a member who has committed a public sin. As a result, people have begun to believe we can overlook sin.

Yet the church has a God-given responsibility to judge certain sins. If you have any doubts about this, read the following passage:

> Your boasting is not good. Don't you know that a little yeast works through the whole batch of dough? Get rid of the old yeast that you may be a new batch without yeast—as you really are. For Christ, our Passover lamb, has been sacrificed. Therefore let us keep the Festival, not with the old yeast, the yeast of malice and wickedness, but with bread without yeast, the bread of sincerity and truth. I have written you in my letter not to associate with sexually immoral people—not at all meaning the people of this world who are immoral, or the greedy and swindlers, or idolaters. In that case you would have to leave this world. But now I am writing you that you must not associate with anyone who calls himself a brother but is sexually immoral or greedy, an idolater or a slanderer, a drunkard or a swindler. With such a man do not even eat. What business is it of mine to judge those outside the church? Are you not to judge those inside? God will judge those outside. "Expel the wicked man from among you" (1 Cor. 5:6–13).

The church is supposed to judge sins that dishonor the name of Christ. When a member commits such sins, it is the duty of the church—in Jesus' name—to take disciplinary action.

Scripture teaches that biblical discipline serves two purposes. First, the individual who is disciplined needs to be restored to fellowship with God and the local church. A person who commits a sin that dishonors the name of Christ has lost the joy of the Holy Spirit. Until the person is broken, repents, and asks for forgiveness and restoration, he or she cannot be filled with the Holy Spirit. That person is out of fellowship with God and cannot be used by Him.

Second, biblical discipline instills the fear of God in a congregation. The church is not a country club where anything goes. The church is the house of God. People need to know that no one can play games with God.

When we ignore the public sin of our fellow believers, we give the impression that sin isn't so bad after all. We must affirm, by loving discipline, that a man or woman cannot carry a Bible around, claim to be a believer, then openly sin and get away with it. When a congregation practices biblical discipline, its members become aware of God's unwavering judgment of sin and His unfailing forgiveness of the repentant sinner.

Of course, there are right and wrong ways to judge. The Bible clearly states, "Do not judge, or you too will be judged" (Matt. 7:1). This passage often is used as an excuse not to exercise biblical discipline. However, it refers to judging a person's motivation, which is none of our business. First Corinthians 5 has nothing to do with judging another's motivation—but has everything to do with judging a person's obvious conduct. The Bible says we are to separate ourselves from anyone who practices these outward sins and still claims to be a believer. Not only are we to separate ourselves individually, but also as a church we are actively to discipline that person.

The biblical teaching on discipline is outlined in Matthew 18:15–17. First, we are to approach the person who has sinned. If the person won't listen, we are to take two or three others with us and try again. If the person still doesn't listen, we are to bring the person before the congregation so that the elders, on behalf of the congregation, may take disciplinary action.

As difficult as such action may be, it is not cruel; it is the kindest thing we can do for a person. Such action enables a person to see how serious his or her sin is and opens the door to repentance. If a person is not repentant, does not want to be restored to fellowship, and withdraws from the church, however, the church has no basis for discipline.

A woman in Oklahoma successfully sued her former church because it persisted in disciplining her after she withdrew from fellowship. The church elders, exercising their scriptural responsibility, had confronted this member about her admitted immoral behavior. They told her she would be disciplined before the congregation if she did not repent. They also asked members of the church to encourage her to repent.

Up to this point, the elders' actions were appropriate and necessary. The woman needed to repent so she could be restored to full fellowship in the church. But when the woman withdrew from fellowship, restoration no longer was possible. Instead of exposing the woman's immoral behavior to the congregation (which led to the lawsuit), the elders should have dropped the issue, realizing that further discipline would not result in restoration.

The church cannot discipline people who do not want fellowship in the church. We must never forget that the purpose of discipline is not to put down the sinner, but to restore that person to fellowship.

Discipline is necessary to awaken people to their sin so they can repent and be restored. God does not deal with sin by covering it up. God exposes sin and forgives it, releasing us from Satan's deadly grasp. The person who has unconfessed sin in his or her life is in Satan's grasp until the matter is cleared up.

Satan is like a gossipy newspaper columnist who points to your past sins. He says, "You'd better march to my tune or I'll let the world know all about you." Or he's like a business partner who knows you have made some shady deals. If you don't meet his demands, he will destroy you by exposing your evil deeds.

God demands that the church exercise biblical discipline because it enables us to be completely free from our sin and walk in His light. When properly executed, biblical discipline does not destroy people, but releases them from Satan's destruction by producing conviction, sorrow, repentance, and—most important—restoration.

DISCIPLINE IS PAINFUL

Discipline of any kind hurts. Discipline in the church is even more difficult because it involves disciplining someone we love very much.

Biblical discipline is painful not only for the guilty person, but also for the whole congregation. Paul expresses the extent of the pain of discipline: "If anyone has caused grief, he has not so much grieved me as he has grieved all of you, to some extent—not to put it too severely" (2 Cor. 2:5).

Yes, discipline hurts so much that we grope for excuses not to apply it. We say, "Well, who are we to judge? It could happen to us, too." Or, "Isn't it cruel to discipline someone? Won't it hurt?"

Although discipline hurts us deeply, Scripture says that when we follow the Lord's command and exercise discipline, we're not being cruel. Instead, we are being loving. It is far more cruel to neglect this responsibility than to follow through with the restorative, though painful, process of discipline.

Which is more cruel? To permit the situation to deteriorate to gossip, or for the church to take action and attempt to restore a man or woman to fellowship through biblical discipline, which exposes the sin and can lead people to brokenness, repentance, and forgiveness?

DISCIPLINE LEADS TO FORGIVENESS AND RESTORATION

As heartbreaking as it may be, biblical discipline doesn't end with a broken spirit. A person who is broken and confesses his or her sin can be forgiven and restored to fellowship. When that person is restored, great rejoicing should follow. Read Paul's instructions to the Corinthians regarding their forgiveness of the repentant sinner in their fellowship:

> The punishment inflicted on him by the majority is sufficient for him. Now instead, you ought to forgive and comfort him, so that he will not be overwhelmed by excessive sorrow. I urge you, therefore, to reaffirm your love for him (2 Cor. 2:6–8).

Although this man had sinned openly and could have been arrogant and rebellious when the church called him to discipline, he actually was overwhelmed with grief. His grief proved that he was a true believer.

When Paul learned of the man's repentance, he wrote to the Corinthians, in effect telling them, "Quickly restore the man before he dies from sorrow. He is so broken over his sin that it's going to kill him! Pick him up! Forgive him! Bring him back into the fellowship of the body of

Christ!" This is what biblical discipline is all about. It causes us to realize the consequences of our sin. It humbles us before God and the body of Christ so we can be forgiven and restored to fellowship.

No matter how hard it is to take, discipline is medicine for the soul. Loving, biblical discipline brings healing. It doesn't cover up the sin and allow it to grow like a cancer. Discipline uncovers the sin and allows the blood of Jesus to do its cleansing work. When biblical discipline is practiced, hope and forgiveness replace despair and guilt. If the sinner is proud and arrogant, however, no forgiveness or healing can occur. As Corrie ten Boom often said, "The blood of Jesus never cleansed an excuse."

I'd like to share a contemporary example of biblical discipline and restoration. A Christian woman in Argentina had been widowed for about three years. She was almost forty and had several children. Then she met a man who said that he too was widowed. They began dating, attended church together, and eventually decided to marry.

Everything went smoothly until a few weeks before the wedding when, in a moment of passion, they had intimate relations. The woman subsequently became pregnant, and three days before the wedding her fiancé disappeared. He left a note explaining his actions:

"I'm terribly sorry to tell you this, but I was not truthful with you when I said I was a widower—I had a wife all along. During the two years we've been going together I have been trying to legalize my divorce. I thought I'd be able to dissolve the marriage, but I couldn't. I'm very sorry, but I have to leave."

Naturally, the woman was devastated. She not only had been betrayed by the man she loved, but also had committed an immoral act.

About a year after the baby was born, the woman moved to a larger city and began attending a church that celebrated the Lord's Supper. The woman went to every service, but always sat in the back, weeping, and refrained from participating in the Lord's Supper.

The elders noticed her behavior and went to visit her. They told her they were delighted she was attending their church, but were concerned about her sadness. They wanted to know why she did not participate in the Lord's Supper. "I deserve to be disciplined," she said. "I cannot take the Lord's Supper because I have dishonored the Lord." She then told them her whole story.

Recognizing her need for discipline, the elders asked, "Would you like us to discipline you properly, then bring you back into fellowship?"

"Yes," she said, "I really would."

The following Sunday, the elders brought the matter before the congregation. The elders explained, without telling all the details, that the woman had experienced a moral failure in her life. "She is repentant and has asked us to exercise biblical discipline," they said. "So we will wait a few weeks. If we see continued repentance in this sister, we want to forgive her and quickly restore her to the full fellowship of this church." Everyone in the congregation was crying; they were distressed about what had happened and hurt deeply for their sister in Christ.

About six weeks later, the elders again addressed the congregation. "Our sister," they said, "as you have seen, has been humbled. She is broken and repentant. We have forgiven her for her past failing and now restore her to the fellowship of the church. We want her to participate in the Lord's Supper and would like her to teach a girls' Sunday School class."

All that happened many years ago. This woman went to be with the Lord recently, but for the rest of her life, only a handful of people knew about her failing. Not because it was covered up, but because biblical discipline and restoration took place. Instead of being consumed by guilt, the woman and her family were able to live without shame or embarrassment. Sure, the discipline was difficult. It hurt. The woman was humbled. She was broken. Sadness filled the church during her period of discipline. But she was restored. She lived happily in the Lord. She actively served the Lord, winning people to Jesus Christ. This is the kind of complete healing biblical discipline brings!

FORGIVENESS PREVENTS DESPAIR

As the previous story indicates, when a person repents and asks to be forgiven for his or her sin, the church has both the responsibility and authority to forgive. Paul sets the example for us by saying, "If you forgive anyone, I also forgive him" (2 Cor. 2:10). When giving His Sermon on the Mount (Matt. 6:14–15), Jesus said that whoever we forgive on earth, God in heaven will forgive. Forgiveness is a God-given right and responsibility to be used to restore those who have fallen. We act under God's authority when we practice biblical discipline.

Paul goes on to explain why forgiveness is so important: "And what I have forgiven—if there was anything to forgive—I have forgiven in the sight of Christ for your sake, in order that Satan might not outwit us. For we are not unaware of his schemes" (2 Cor. 2:10-11).

Discipline is not supposed to overwhelm a person with excessive despair, which is of Satan. Instead, biblical discipline is to create a godly sorrow that will lead to repentance, forgiveness, and enable the church to restore the sinner to fellowship. When someone obviously is broken and repentant, the church must stand up and say, "In the name of the Lord Jesus, rejoice! He has forgiven you and we forgive you too."

We know that God forgives us, but we need to know that our brothers and sisters forgive us too. The assurance of corporate forgiveness and restoration to fellowship brings healing, joy, and purity to the entire congregation.

One reason church discipline is out of favor today is because the church has not always practiced loving, biblical discipline. In the past, the church sometimes threatened its straying members behind closed doors; this led to anger, rather than restoration. At other times, the church forgot that forgiveness was part of discipline. Instead of disciplining people in order to lift them up, forgive them, and restore them, the church hit them so hard they became absolutely despondent.

For example, how many divorced men and women dared to enter an evangelical church thirty or forty years ago? Very few. Divorced men and women often were spiritually clobbered by those who considered themselves more righteous. We still have more to learn about ministering to people whose marriages have been broken, but some churches now have gone to the other extreme. They are so lenient that they ignore the affairs or abusive behavior of their members. In doing so, they hurt the family who desperately needs the church's loving support.

It is precisely when the church does not forgive and quickly restore a repentant member to fellowship that Satan schemes to destroy that person. Satan whispers to the repentant person, "Look, there's nothing good about that church. They don't love you. Look how miserable you are because of their discipline. You've confessed and asked for forgiveness, but they only want to crush you."

Rather than create an atmosphere in which Satan can destroy a brother or sister, the body of Christ has a unique opportunity to build up and restore each member. Love demands that we allow a person to be free from his or her haunting past. A disciplined, forgiven person is free. Such a person can confidently move on in life, knowing that God does not remember a sin confessed (Heb. 10:17).

A man in Guatemala who had dishonored the name of our Lord was truly broken and had repented, but still had no joy. He desperately needed reassurance from the body of Christ that he was forgiven. Realizing his despair and need for restoration, I did something that his own church should have done. Putting my arm around him I said, "Brother, you've repented. Your sins have been forgiven by God. Christ's blood has set you free from your sin. May we pray together?"

That humble man was ecstatic. "Thank you, thank you, thank you," he cried. With tears streaming down his face, he gave me such a big hug I thought I would suffocate. What a thrill it was to see his joy return because he had been reassured of his forgiveness! Although such a situation is an exception to the rule, it illustrates our need to take restoration seriously.

DISCIPLINE IS AN ACT OF OBEDIENCE

The church needs to practice loving biblical discipline not only because it produces healing, but also because it reflects obedience to God. Paul explains, "The reason I wrote you was to see if you would stand the test and be obedient in everything" (2 Cor. 2:9).

Biblical discipline is not done out of spite or for the self-righteous satisfaction of others. It is not the self-serving policy of one church or denomination. Rather, biblical discipline is done in love as an act of obedience to God.

We can't play around with sin in the body of Christ. We must deal with it seriously, as God demands. God commands us to lift up our fallen brother or sister, to clear the name of Christ, and to proclaim the meaning of holiness. This is accomplished only through loving, obedient discipline. When a church takes biblical discipline seriously, cleansing and healing result.

DISOBEDIENCE HURTS THOUSANDS

Disobedience and delay in exercising biblical discipline, however, hurts thousands of people. This was true in the Corinthian church, and is true today. While Paul was trying to deal with the Corinthians' discipline problem, his ministry came to a halt. Read his analysis of the situation:

> Now when I went to Troas to preach the gospel of Christ and
> found that the Lord had opened a door for me, I still had no peace
> of mind, because I did not find my brother Titus there. So I said good-
> by to them and went to Macedonia (2 Cor. 2:12–13).

It's easy to imagine Paul's enthusiasm about the opportunity to preach in Troas. Troas was without a church and the door was wide open to receive the Gospel. When Paul arrived there, he expected to meet Titus and begin evangelistic work. But Titus never showed up, indicating that the problem in Corinth was even more serious than Paul had thought. This tore Paul up inside. He couldn't even function. Instead of taking advantage of the opportunity to preach, he left the city and headed for Macedonia to wait for Titus.

It's difficult to know how much Troas suffered because of the delayed obedience in Corinth. Scripture doesn't indicate that a church ever flourished in Troas, and we don't know how long Troas remained open to the Gospel. We do know that Paul was unable to seize the opportunity at hand. Because a church failed to discipline a member of its congregation in a quick manner, the ministry of the Gospel suffered in a city hundreds of miles away.

This isn't the only example of the harmful effects of disobedience to God recorded in the Bible. Do you remember what happened to Joshua and the Israelites after the battle of Jericho? God commanded the Israelites not to touch any property in Jericho. But one man, Achan, broke that command (Josh. 7:1). So when the Israelites fought their next battle, which should have been an easy victory, they suffered a terrible loss.

Joshua was shocked! He went to the Lord in prayer, asking why God had allowed such a defeat. God's response was, "Get up. I don't want any crying or weeping. Sin is in your midst! Cleanse out the sin and you shall have victory again." Although Israel as a nation had not sinned, the sin of one member had robbed the nation of its holiness, rendering its actions ineffective.

We easily forget that our actions, like those of Achan or the people of Corinth, affect many others—especially other members of the body of Christ. When we fail to deal with public sin in a biblical way, we hurt many people. We don't just hurt members of our immediate family. We hurt members of God's family.

Satan laughs when we persist in making excuses for our sin. We are fooling ourselves if we think we can accomplish the work of God when unresolved sin places us under Satan's control. We must obey God's command and practice loving biblical discipline in order to be cleansed and forgiven. Only when we are restored to fellowship with God and our fellow believers will we begin to live a life of joy and holiness!

FOR PERSONAL REFLECTION

Read 2 Corinthians 1:23–2:13.

1. "Sin kills joy and the joy of the Spirit can be regained only when that person is restored to fellowship with God." Have you experienced a time when unconfessed sin killed your joy in Christ? How does public sin affect a person's relationship with both God and other believers?

2. "For I wrote you . . . not to grieve you but to let you know the depth of my love for you" (2 Cor. 2:4). How did Paul express his great love for the Corinthian believers in this messy situation? What motivates your response to people who are openly sinning or refusing to deal with public sin? How would that be expressed?

3. "God does not deal with sin by covering it up." How does exposing—instead of hiding—sin bring freedom and healing? Why does God choose to deal with sin openly instead of just ignoring it?

4. "We know that God forgives us, but we need to know that our brothers and sisters forgive us too." How should you respond to a person who has sincerely repented? How can your expression of forgiveness minister to him or her?

FOR INTERACTIVE DISCUSSION

Read aloud 2 Corinthians 1:23–2:13.

1. Read 1 Corinthians 5:1–13. "As shocking as this act of immorality was, the Corinthians' complacent attitude toward the sinners distressed Paul even more." Why was this so? Why did Paul rebuke them so severely?

2. "The Corinthian church finally recognized its disobedience and obeyed Paul's admonition." How did they discipline the sinning man? How did he respond?

3. "What do you think your church would have done in this situation?" How has your church community dealt with public, flagrant sin? What other kinds of public sins demand this kind of serious attention?

4. "Scripture teaches that biblical discipline serves two purposes." What are these two purposes? What else does biblical discipline accomplish?

5. "Of course, there are right and wrong ways to judge." How does exercising biblical discipline differ from obeying Jesus' command to "judge not" (Matt. 7:1)?

6. Read Matthew 18:15–17. What is the progression for dealing with flagrant sin? How does this work in today's world? What are some important principles to consider when applying biblical discipline?

7. "Loving, biblical discipline brings healing." Why is this true?

CHAPTER 6

Living a Victorious Christian Life

I wonder why it is," an Anglican bishop once pondered, "that everywhere the Apostle Paul went they had a revolution, and everywhere I go they serve a cup of tea?"

Unfortunately, many Christians today live lives with even less impact than that bishop's. In fact, we sometimes equate victorious Christian living with an untroubled life. So when the going gets rough—when we suffer financial setbacks, when our kids get into trouble, when we succumb to serious illness, or when we're out of work—we begin to think something's wrong with us spiritually. Why? Because we no longer seem to be living the life we thought strong Christians lived.

We often look to the Apostle Paul as a model of a Christian living in victory. But that didn't make his life a breeze. He often was in trouble or embroiled in controversy. During his first missionary journey, Paul was stoned and left for dead. During his second missionary journey, he eluded arrest on charges of turning the world upside down. Throughout his life, Paul experienced incredible hardship: imprisonment, beatings, lashings, shipwrecks, destitution, and exhaustion. Yet he remained optimistic; he lived in victory. Even in jail he wrote, "Rejoice in the Lord always. I will say it again: Rejoice!" (Phil. 4:4).

For some reason we like to think that Paul never made a mistake. But he did. Paul certainly wasn't perfect. Earlier, we saw that he was so pre-occupied with the problems in Corinth that he couldn't take advantage of the evangelistic opportunity in Troas (2 Cor. 2:12–13). Later, Paul must have been grieved when he looked back on that missed opportunity. Yet he was able to go on, joyfully triumphant in Christ. Paul had an inde-structible optimism that enabled him to say, "But thanks be to God, who always leads us in triumphal procession in Christ" (2:14). What optimism! What victory! Isn't this the kind of victory every believer longs for? It's hard to imagine how Paul managed to live with a joyous confidence as he did. Yet triumph in Christ often is more visible when trouble comes to us and the reality of our faith is tested.

In this passage Paul explains the basic truths of triumphant Christian living that revolutionized my life. Although I began learning these lessons long ago, I often have to remind myself of them. I still find myself saying, "In spite of all the problems, in spite of the plans that fall apart, thanks be to God who in Christ Jesus always leads us in triumph!"

HOW CAN A CHRISTIAN BE VICTORIOUS?

Learning what joy, optimism, and victory in the Christian life are all about wasn't easy for me. When I became a believer I learned about forgiveness and never really doubted that God had forgiven me. But I didn't understand much about how a Christian progressed in maturity and holiness. I longed to get past the continual struggles and find vic-tory in my life.

I wasn't alone in my desire for greater victory. The other young men I spent time with wanted victory too. And we needed it! We had many weaknesses. We made sarcastic remarks, despised certain denominations, and had our temptations with women—just to name a few. So whenev-er a big-name preacher came to our church for revival services, we would take him out for coffee and ask him how we could have victory in our lives. We never told him too much about our reason for wanting greater victo-ry; we just hinted that we had some little weaknesses in our lives.

Every one of those preachers gave us the same answer. "Well, are you reading the Bible?" they would ask.

"Yes, we read the Bible," we replied—and we were dedicated in our Bible reading. We underlined verses, memorized passages, and got up early so we could read the Bible before going to work. But nothing clicked.

Sometimes we were ecstatic, feeling as though we had victory; at other times we were dragging, feeling so unspiritual.

After hearing our response, every one of the preachers would say, "Well, read some more. And pray."

The truth was, we already were praying quite a bit. Every morning we prayed on our knees by our beds. Yet we wondered, *How long do we have to pray before something happens?* We were so eager to be holy that we prayed together on Friday nights. But by the next week, we would have to do it all over again.

So we told these preachers how much we read the Bible and prayed. Then they would ask, "Are you working for the Lord?"

Did we work for the Lord! We handed out ten tracts a day. On weekends we held street meetings and children's classes.

We preached every opportunity we had. But something still was missing. We prayed more, read more, and worked more, but inside we were spiritual wrecks.

As I look back on that time, I realize the counsel we received actually weakened us. We failed to live the victorious Christian life for the same reason many others are failing today. Unconsciously, we were trying to produce spiritual growth and strength through our own ability and power, instead of relying on the living Christ who leads us in triumph. Over and over we were told to read the Bible, pray every day, and work for Christ. If we did those things, our advisers promised, we would be happy, holy Christians.

The truth is, though those three activities are important, they are not enough. Of course victorious Christians pray. Of course victorious Christians read the Bible. Of course victorious Christians work for the Lord. But what we do is not the real basis for victory in the Christian life. It is not the basis for authenticity.

When I was young and searching for victory, no one ever told me that. Not one of those great men of God ever said, "Listen, the secret is not reading, praying, and working. The secret is that Christ lives in you. All of the wisdom, power, and resources of Jesus Christ are available to you because He lives in you."

The secret of victory—the indestructible optimism that Paul exhibited in his life, and which we long for today—is not what *we do for Christ* but what *He does through us!* When we abide in Christ, and our relationship with Him is the most important part of our lives, He will bring us into authentic victory.

Struggling to achieve victory through our own efforts often can leave us cynical. I will never forget an experience I had as a young man in Argentina. As I searched a bookstore for a book on victory, a man I highly respected walked in and asked, "Hey, Luis, what are you looking for?"

I had just picked up a book by Norman Grubb and I said, "Man, I want victory. Someone told me this book by Norman Grubb is great. I can't wait to read it."

"Oh, yeah, victory, victory, victory," he sneered. "I'd like to put Norman Grubb under a car with a flat tire in the middle of the desert and see what he says about victory!"

That remark threw cold water on my search for victory for some time. But eventually, I began to learn what victory is, to discover the real basis of triumph. I began to see the difference between struggling to achieve spiritual success on my own, and living an authentic life of obedience as a natural result of following Christ. I had to learn that what God would do *through* me was far greater than what I could do *for* Him.

PRAISE AND THANKSGIVING ARE PART OF VICTORY

Second Corinthians 2:14 begins with a note of praise: "Thanks be to God," Paul says, "who always leads us in triumphal procession in Christ." Praise and thanksgiving are essential to authentic Christian living!

During my missionary internship period, when I studied under the late Fred Renich, I began to see how positive prayers of praise and victory affected my attitude and the way I lived. During class one day, Fred asked, "What kind of prayers do you start your day with? Are your prayers negative and depressing, or are your prayers positive, affirming God's promises?

"Do you get up and praise God for what He is going to do in your life? Do you say, 'Thank You, Lord Jesus, for this new day. Thank You that although I may face troubles today, You will never leave me nor forsake me because You live within me. Thank You that You are greater than any opposition I might face today. Thank You that although I may be tempted today, You are more powerful than any temptation'?

"Or do you say, 'O Lord, I feel miserable. Please help me get through this day. I know I won't make it on my own. And if I have to witness to anyone, You know I won't know what to say, so please help me'?"

When he finished speaking, I realized that although I loved the Word and loved to pray, I always began my day with a self-centered, negative prayer, knowing that I would fail. So from then on I tried to begin each day with a prayer of confidence in God. I would get up and say, "Thank You, Lord Jesus, that I am alive and well. It's a new day. In spite of my weaknesses, You will give me strength. Although I'm tired, You will give me energy. In spite of the problems I may face, You will help me solve them. When I have an opportunity to serve You, You will give me wisdom and courage. Thank You, Lord, that You indwell me. Thank You for the victories of this day."

When I start the day with a positive, joyful prayer to the Lord as the Apostle Paul prayed, I even can be with people who are negative without becoming negative myself. But if I don't start with a note of joy and optimism, I am easily dragged down by any negative person around me.

But notice that this indestructible optimism isn't just wishy-washy positive thinking. This isn't the type of positive thinking that comes from standing in front of a mirror and saying, "I feel great! I feel fine! I feel terrific!" That's *not* what Paul is talking about. Paul is talking about the biblical confidence and hope that comes from knowing we dwell in the risen Christ, who always leads us in triumph. Our ability to overcome and grow through the challenges of life doesn't come from being positive thinkers or having a sanguine temperament, but because we are in Jesus Christ. That makes all the difference.

Paul describes the dynamic experience of living in the power of the indwelling Christ: "I have been crucified with Christ and I no longer live, but Christ lives in me. The life I live in the body, I live by faith in the Son of God, who loved me and gave himself for me" (Gal. 2:20). That's the source of a Christian's authentic optimism.

Realizing that victory did not depend on what I accomplished, but on who I was in Christ, revolutionized my life! Suddenly I realized that sweating it out for Christ wasn't going to bring me victory. Victory would result when I followed Him in prayer and obedience.

Because I was in the habit of thinking about what I could do for God, it took me a long time to learn that Christ was working in me, through me, and for me. Years later, I'm still learning what it means to rest in the indwelling Christ, allowing Him to have His way in me, knowing that He will do far more through me than I could ever do on my own.

CHRIST LEADS US IN TRIUMPH

Before I began to learn what true victory and authentic spiritual growth was, my spiritual life had all the stability of a roller coaster. If I attended a Bible conference that featured a good speaker, I was up. I felt like a jet taking off on a clear day. But after a few days, I always came in for a crash landing. I would just drag myself along until the next great speaker showed up; then I would take in what he said and be off and running again.

It was like being tied to a carousel horse: the music sounds like a stuck accordion, the horses go up and down and round and round, and if you stay on the thing too long, you go crazy. Yet thousands of Christians are stuck on the same spiritual carousel I was—and it's driving them crazy. Their spiritual lives are wrecked, their homes are failing, and a great pain dwells within the body of Christ.

The reason for this heartache and turmoil is that we have forgotten a key word that Paul uses in his statement of victory—the word *triumph*. How could Paul say that Christ always leads us in triumph? Hadn't Paul just blown a fantastic opportunity to preach the Gospel in Troas? Didn't he deeply regret that failing? Yes, Paul had blown it. Yes, he did regret it. But in spite of his failing he was able to continue because Christ was leading him.

Paul knew the Christian life is meant to be steady and balanced, even in the midst of trouble, because Christ always leads us. On our own we aren't steady, balanced characters. We can do nothing apart from Him (John 15:5). But when we abide in Him, the indwelling Christ makes us balanced people.

Not only does Christ always lead us, but Paul says He also leads us in triumph. This means that though we encounter battles, temptations, and troubles, Christ will give us the victory—the ability to come out the other side more Christ-centered and mature in our understanding and our responses. His power makes us successful!

Our success, however, isn't necessarily what the world calls success—fame, good health, wealth—although nothing is wrong with that kind of success. Our success in Christ is spiritual success, which I believe Henrietta Mears defines better than anyone: "Success is anything that is pleasing to Him." Christ guarantees that He will lead us to success in anything that pleases Him. So it's important to know how He enables us to have victory and success in the midst of difficult circumstances.

How Christ Leads Us in Triumph

First, when we allow the indwelling Christ to control us, we have the mind of Christ. The mind of Christ transforms our desires, ambitions, and thought patterns so that we begin to think the thoughts of the Lord. Even though we face temptations, the Lord can lead us in victory because His thoughts become our thoughts. His desires become our desires.

Second, we have victory in Christ because He gives us a love of holiness. This love of holiness is a work of the indwelling Christ, because by nature we don't love holiness. But when we allow Christ to control us, He provides this love and desire. It is not a put-on, but our authentic desire and identity.

Third, Christ gives us the power to implement both His thoughts and His love of holiness. When we face temptation, we can turn to the indwelling Christ and say, "Lord Jesus, I can't handle this temptation alone, but I thank You that Your power is more than sufficient. Thank You for helping me overcome this temptation." Christ's power to overcome temptation is real when we allow Him to be in control.

Fourth, when we fail, the blood of Jesus Christ cleanses us from all sin. We don't have to remain fallen. When we stumble and fall, He cleanses us so we can be victorious again. We cannot afford to forget that He cleanses and restores us on the spot, for if we refuse His cleansing and allow sin to accumulate, it will be impossible for us to overcome temptation. But whenever we seek Him after a fall, He will cleanse us and lead us in triumph.

We Are the Fragrance of Christ

Any believer who lives a life of victory and success carries the fragrance, or influence, of Christ to other people. The Apostle Paul carried the fragrance of Christ with him. Wherever he went, he influenced people. Some loved him; others hated him. But one thing was certain: they couldn't ignore him—or his God. The fragrance of the living Christ, who lived within Paul, permeated the air around him.

Paul describes the fragrance of Christ and its work in terms that border on the poetic:

> But thanks be to God, who always leads us in triumphal procession in Christ and through us spreads everywhere the fragrance of the knowledge of him. For we are to God the aroma of Christ among those

who are being saved and those who are perishing. To the one we are the smell of death; to the other, the fragrance of life. And who is equal to such a task? (2 Cor. 2:14–16).

Notice the phrase "through us spreads everywhere the fragrance." When we walk in the control of the indwelling Christ, He spreads His fragrance to the world around us.

When I think of the fragrance of Christ, I picture being in an elevator with a person who's wearing a distinctive perfume or cologne. Everyone immediately notices that person, and long after the person leaves, the fragrance lingers. So it is with the authentic Christian. The divine presence of the Lord Jesus within a Christian is a dynamic element that others notice and do not easily forget.

Have you ever met a person who truly walks each day with the Lord? Isn't it a beautiful thing? When you're with that person, you sense the aroma of Jesus Christ. You love to be with that person. Even talking about unimportant things is a blessing when you're with him or her because the presence of Jesus Christ is at work.

Years ago, when I was a teenager in Argentina, I had the privilege of meeting some people like that. On Tuesdays, which were prayer nights at our church, I would go directly to church from work. Though I'd get there early, there would always be a small group of elderly women and men already praying. It was a great delight to sit with them and ask them questions. Those people were not theologians. In fact, some of them were illiterate. But because Jesus Christ controlled their lives, they made an unforgettable impression on me.

As I travel the world today, I catch that fragrance in the lives of many people I meet. Whether they are students in China or retirees in Florida, people high up on the social ladder with great political influence or husbands and wives reaching out to their neighbors next door, if they are deeply in love with Jesus and living for Him—it's an aroma that can't be missed.

The fragrance of Christ is not something we can manufacture or gain through education. It is totally God's doing. When we walk transparently in the power and presence of the indwelling Christ, His perfume envelops us and spreads to others. No matter what we do, where we go, who we talk with, or who we do business with, the Lord uses us for His glory to spread His fragrance throughout the world.

The fragrance of Christ isn't something we can turn on or turn off. We can't consciously say, "I must act like a Christian so I can spread Christ's fragrance." Rather, Christ's perfume spreads to others even when we are unaware of it. We don't have to worry whether the fragrance is flowing, because when we walk with Him, it will flow automatically. Our responsibility is simply to walk in fellowship with the indwelling Christ.

One evening, while dining in a restaurant with members of my evangelistic team, I saw a beautiful example of how the fragrance of Christ works. Perhaps you've had a similar experience. Several couples were seated at the table next to us. One man in that group arrived after the others, but before he sat down, he gave one of the other men a big hug. I thought to myself, *Those two guys really love each other. I bet they're Christians.* When the meal was served, they all held hands and prayed.

Afterward we talked with them and learned that they were indeed Christians. But even before I saw them pray or had the opportunity to speak with them, I had been blessed by watching them talk and laugh together (and I'm a tough fellow to bless). While they were enjoying their time together, the perfume of Christ was flowing. They weren't trying to impress anyone. They just were being themselves—and the perfume was flowing. To us who were saved, we recognized the aroma of Christ.

Sometimes, the person who is wearing the perfume becomes accustomed to it and doesn't even realize how others are affected.

Chuck Colson, the founder of Prison Fellowship, tells a story of standing in a long line in an airport on a hot, steamy day in Jakarta. After the all-night flight, he was tired and irritated on the inside, but he must have kept his cool because later he received a letter from a senior partner in a major Singapore law firm. Unbeknownst to Colson, this man had been watching him.

The man, who was of Chinese ancestry and grew up with a Confucian background, had no involvement in the Christian church. But, several years before, wanting some moral training for his children, he had enrolled them in Sunday school at a church. One day his children brought home Chuck Colson's autobiography, *Born Again,* which featured the author's profile on the book jacket. That day in the airport in Jakarta, the Chinese lawyer recognized Colson as the man on the book. He determined that, when he got home, he would read that book about that fellow who was waiting so patiently in line.

Two years later, the man wrote to thank Colson for being in Indonesia and not losing his cool in those long lines at the airport. His demonstration of patience impressed this man, who gave his life to Jesus Christ after reading *Born Again*.

Was Chuck Colson standing in that line forcing himself to act like a good Christian because someone might be watching? No. He was living out his daily life in dependence upon Christ. He displayed patience as part of the Spirit's work in his life—and that aroma of Christ wafted over to a watching man in the other line, who was being saved as a result

THE FRAGRANCE OF CHRIST HAS A SPECIAL PURPOSE

Sometimes, we don't see the results of Christ's fragrance. We may wonder if it's really worthwhile to proclaim the name of Jesus. But if we look again at a key verse, we'll see an important purpose for the fragrance of Christ: "For we are to God the aroma of Christ among . . . those who are perishing" (2 Cor. 2:15). In other words, the fragrance of Christ doesn't spread out into the world just to linger there. Its purpose is to bring people to Jesus Christ. And even those who reject Christ cannot escape the impact of that aroma.

A story about Frederick S. Arnot, the great missionary to Africa in the late nineteenth century, helps to remind me that the fragrance of Christ is doing its work even when we don't see results.

Arnot went with a friend to preach in the tavern district of his hometown in Scotland. They stood on a street corner and sang a few hymns to gather a crowd. While Frederick and his friend were singing, the crowd was silent, but as soon as they began to speak about their faith in Christ, the crowd booed and jeered so loudly they couldn't be heard.

So Frederick and his friend began singing again. When the crowd quieted down, they tried to preach again, but once more were overwhelmed by shouts and taunts.

This happened several times. Frederick loved the Lord and desperately wanted to share the Good News with the crowd, but they would not hear him.

Finally, tears in his eyes, he bowed his head in defeat and started to walk away with his friend. Perhaps he felt that his preaching was only "the smell of death" to those who are perishing. But he had taken only a few steps when he felt a hand on his shoulder. He turned and faced a tall, elderly stranger. The old man looked him in the eye and said, "Keep at it, laddie; God loves to hear men speak well of His Son!"

That was all the encouragement Frederick needed. He went back to that corner, and the crowd, moved by his courage, finally began to listen.

In any century, God loves to hear us speak well of His Son. That's the perfume. That's the precious aroma we give to God. That's a natural result of dwelling in Christ—of living authentic lives in dependency on Him!

FOR PERSONAL REFLECTION

Read 2 Corinthians 2:14–16

1. "In fact, we sometimes equate victorious Christian living with an untroubled life." What is your concept of victorious Christian living? How does this compare with Paul's understanding and experience of authentic victory?

2. "I began to see the difference between struggling to achieve spiritual success on my own, and living an authentic life of obedience as a natural result of following Christ." Have you ever had a checklist for achieving spiritual success? What was on it? How does that contrast with authentic obedience? Which is more true of your life?

3. "Praise and thanksgiving are essential to authentic Christian living!" What part do praise and thanksgiving play in your life? How can joyful, positive prayer change your outlook and experience?

4. "Before I began to learn what true victory and authentic spiritual growth was, my spiritual life had all the stability of a roller coaster." Have you ever been on a "spiritual roller-coaster ride?" What would it take to "get off"?

5. "When we walk transparently in the power and presence of the indwelling Christ, His perfume envelops us and spreads to others." How does living in constant dependency on Christ free you to be who you are in Him, yet powerfully impact those around you? What kind of aroma do others receive from your life?

FOR INTERACTIVE DISCUSSION

Read aloud 2 Corinthians 2:14–16

1. "What optimism! What victory! Isn't this the kind of victory that every believer longs for?" What do most people expect from their Christian life? How does this compare with Paul's experience? What kind of victory do you long for in your life?

2. "Triumph in Christ often is more visible when trouble comes to us and the reality of our faith is tested." What kind of troubles in Paul's life revealed Christ's triumph? What was his response? How can you see Christ leading you in triumph in the midst of your personal difficulties?

3. "I realize the counsel we received actually weakened us." What kind of counsel would you give a young believer desiring to live an authentic, victorious Christian life?

4. "But notice that this indestructible optimism isn't just wishy-washy positive thinking." What *is* the difference between this optimism and wishy-washy positive thinking? How do we encourage optimism instead of cynicism in living the Christian life?

5. "It's important to know how He enables us to have victory and success in the midst of difficult circumstances." What does it mean that Christ leads us in triumph? How does this happen?

6. "The fragrance of Christ isn't something we can turn on or turn off." If the fragrance of Christ doesn't have an on-off switch, how does God spread the knowledge of Christ through us? What part do we play?

CHAPTER 7

Time to Stop Pretending

When Bill Fuqua was fourteen years old, he decided to stand utterly motionless in a public place—just to see what reactions he'd get. His curiosity definitely paid off. One woman, for example, walked by him, stared, then touched him. When her action brought no response, she actually remarked, "Oh, I thought it was a real person!"

Since then, Bill has advanced to the point where he now holds the world's record for doing nothing. On one occasion, he stood motionless for ten hours and six minutes to earn his place in the *Guinness Book of World Records.*

From all appearances, it seems as though some Christians are determined to break Bill Fuqua's record. Too often, Christians stand motionless—doing nothing—when we should be living the victorious Christian life. Instead of spreading the fragrance of Christ, some of us seem trapped in defeat. Why is this so? Why are we unable to allow the indwelling Christ to work through us?

Part of the problem is that some of us have fallen into the trap of pretending to be Christians. We act pious, victorious, and radiant because that is what others expect of us. We probably think God expects us to act that way too. But we aren't being genuine.

Paul attacks this imitation of Christian living: "Unlike so many, we do not peddle the word of God for profit. On the contrary, in Christ we speak before God with sincerity, like men sent from God" (2 Cor. 2:17).

We are not to be peddlers of God's Word. We're not doing a sales pitch for our own personal gain. We are to be sincere, godly people! We are not to put on a show and masquerade as Christians. We are not to depend on our human efforts to live the Christian life. Instead, we are to dwell in Christ and let Him do His work through us.

Inspired by the Holy Spirit, Paul is saying, "Take the mask off! Stop trying to impress others. Stop putting everyone on. Stop covering up your sins. Stop pretending to be a spiritual powerhouse. No one really cares about your show. Walk transparently in Jesus Christ so He can begin to do His work in your life."

We can enjoy the kind of authentic living Paul describes only when we take off our masks and allow Christ to make us the kind of people He wants us to be. We can spread the fragrance of Christ only when we remove our masks so the world can see Christ through us.

DO WE LIVE IN THE SPIRIT OR THE FLESH?

How will we use the hours God has given us? Will we just mark time, feeding ourselves and looking good? Or will we take every opportunity to serve, minister, and lead others to Christ? Will we use the opportunity to minister the life of Christ to others through our own power, or will we do it through the Holy Spirit—in the power of Christ who dwells within us?

Paul clearly identifies the choices Christians must make in order to live and minister effectively through the Holy Spirit (2 Cor. 3:1–4:6). He says we must choose whether we will live in the Spirit or the flesh; whether we will rely on our own limited resources or the unfailing resources of the Spirit; whether we will seek the short-term glory of legalism or the long-term glory of the Spirit; whether we will live transparently or cower behind a veil; and finally, whether we will minister in bold, godly sincerity or as weak imitators of Christ.

Paul addresses the first point—whether we will live in our own power or the unfailing power of the Spirit—in a straightforward fashion:

> Are we beginning to commend ourselves again? Or do we need,
> like some people, letters of recommendation to you or from you? You
> yourselves are our letter, written on our hearts, known and read by

everybody. You show that you are a letter from Christ, the result of our ministry, written not with ink but with the Spirit of the living God, not on tablets of stone but on tablets of human hearts (2 Cor. 3:1–3).

Paul is saying there are two ways to commend ourselves in the ministry. Either we have handwritten approval from man, or divine approval from the Spirit. Our lives show where our approval comes from.

Some churches provide letters of recommendation to members who move to another city and want to join a congregation there. These letters indicate that the person was a member in good standing and are intended to protect the integrity of the Christian community. While few churches observe this practice today, it was done commonly in the early church.

In Paul's case, some of the Corinthians were telling him that if he didn't have a letter of recommendation, he had better not come to Corinth. More than a little surprised at their request, Paul really is saying, "Me? I need a letter of recommendation? You've got to be kidding! *You* are my letter. I led you to Christ. The impact of my life on your life is all the recommendation I need." Paul goes on to say that his letter of recommendation isn't really from him, but from Christ who lives in him.

As Paul points out, either our recommendation comes from the Holy Spirit and reveals the living Christ within us, or it is a shallow, handwritten, human imitation. The theological degrees we may have earned, our baptismal certificates, our ordination papers, or our church membership lists are merely pieces of paper. They say nothing about our effectiveness as Christians. They say no more about our success as Christians than a diploma says about a doctor's skill. Do we choose a doctor on the basis of the medical school he or she attended? Of course not! A doctor's reputation for helping people is the living proof of his or her ability.

Likewise, the impact of our lives on the lives of others is the proof of our ministry. The letter that really counts is the Spirit-written letter. When someone speaks about Christ, even if only briefly, it's easy to tell if that person truly is filled with the Spirit. Of course, some people can put on a good show, but it doesn't take long to see through the façade. A Spirit-filled believer doesn't have to pull out any handwritten letters. Everything about that person gives witness to the indwelling Holy Spirit.

WE ARE COMPETENT TO MINISTER

People who live in the power of Christ are qualified to minister to others. In fact, if we are living an authentic Christian life—revealing the indwelling reality of Christ in all that we say and do—ministry will be the outcome. God doesn't desert us when it comes to ministry. He promises that the Holy Spirit is a more than sufficient resource for any person who gives out and lives out His Word:

> Such confidence as this is ours through Christ before God. Not that we are competent in ourselves to claim anything for ourselves, but our competence comes from God. He has made us competent as ministers of a new covenant—not of the letter but of the Spirit; for the letter kills, but the Spirit gives life (2 Cor. 3:4–6).

We are free to choose whether we will minister through our own resources or through the power of the indwelling Holy Spirit. But who, with any thought, would desire to live and minister with only his or her own strength and resources to draw upon?

Most of us are painfully aware of our failings. We see our spiritual inadequacy all too clearly. This is as it should be. We can give our ministry our best shot, but our best will never be good enough to accomplish anything—not good enough to lead even one person to Christ. We cannot rely on ourselves. But God, through Christ, qualifies us to be ministers of the Good News. Just as we are conscious of our own inadequacy, we must be conscious of the competence God has given us. If Christ lives within us, we have the necessary resources to carry out His ministry. We are sufficient in His sufficiency.

Notice that Paul also says we are ministers of the new covenant—and that is the covenant that gives life. God delivers us from our own inadequacy, granting us tremendous confidence through the Holy Spirit to minister life to others. We don't just preach doctrine. When we live in Christ and depend on His adequacy, we are able to give *life* to others whenever we speak, whenever we share, whenever we encourage, whenever we quote a verse. Every action we do in the power of the Holy Spirit gives life. It's not our ability that gives life; it is the life of Christ flowing through us that brings about blessing and change in those with whom we share our lives.

On one occasion when my evangelistic team and I were in Scotland, two of the team members stayed in a local minister's home. One night they stayed up late, talking with the minister and his wife. In the course of the conversation, the team members mentioned how they came to know Christ.

After everyone else had gone to bed, the minister and his wife talked together. He had been in the ministry for seventeen years, yet he and his wife were not sure they were Christians. The couple talked about their spiritual emptiness and uncertainties for most of the night. They finally decided they would talk with me. They'd ask me how a person could know if he or she were a Christian.

During lunch the next day, the minister and I discussed this question and I had the opportunity to lead him to Christ. He then led his wife and two of their children to Christ. Our team members had not planned to evangelize those people, but the adequacy of Christ was sufficient to bring life to that couple.

As Christians, we are not called to project ourselves. We are called to give out the life of Christ. Our adequacy does not come from intellectual ability or other credentials, although such accomplishments have their place. Our adequacy is of God.

As a part of my ministry, I have the privilege of recording radio programs in English and Spanish that are heard on more than 1,500 stations throughout the United States and Latin America. When I'm sitting in front of the microphone, it would be easy for me to make a quick mental outline of the program and start talking. But I always prepare ahead of time. Hundreds of thousands of people are listening in. And before I begin I pray, "Lord, I don't want to just spout off knowledge. I want to minister life. Take over." Then my ministry becomes a delight because the power of the Holy Spirit is at work.

When we rely on the indwelling Christ, we are never inadequate. We never have to worry whether we'll be able to accomplish the Lord's work. As Paul told the Philippians, "I can do everything through him who gives me strength" (Phil. 4:13). We can be confident and fully sufficient, not in ourselves, but in Christ.

CHOOSING THE PERMANENT GLORY OF CHRIST

The following verses are somewhat difficult to understand. But part of what Paul wants the Corinthians to understand is the two types of glory a Christian can experience:

Now if the ministry that brought death, which was engraved in letters on stone, came with glory, so that the Israelites could not look steadily at the face of Moses because of its glory, fading though it was, will not the ministry of the Spirit be even more glorious? If the ministry that condemns men is glorious, how much more glorious is the ministry that brings righteousness! For what was glorious has no glory now in comparison with the surpassing glory. And if what was fading away came with glory, how much greater is the glory of that which lasts! (2 Cor. 3:7–11).

In other words, Paul says, when trying to live the Christian life, one can experience the glory of the law (legalism) or the permanent glory of the indwelling Christ. When the Apostle Paul refers to the ministry of death, he is referring to the law, or legalism.

You have to admit that legalistic people seem to have a certain amount of glorious splendor. After all, they are disciplined and dedicated to their cause. But legalism always breeds pride. Legalistic people usually look down on those who are less disciplined, less spiritual, less sacrificial, or less dedicated. So the law, or legalism, is in direct contrast to the freedom that comes through the grace of God.

The glory of legalism also fades away because there is a limit to a legalistic person's strength. Eventually, the legalistic person who relies only on human resources will run out of gas. With nothing more to give, he or she falls apart. That's why a person who always has seemed strong and spiritual suddenly may run off with his neighbor's wife. We wonder how such a spiritual man could do that, but the answer may be simple. The man could have been trying to live in his own strength and short-lived glory rather than in the glory of Christ. And as his actions demonstrated, the glory of the law doesn't last.

A few legalistic people manage to hang in there without noticeable failures, but that doesn't mean they won't end up destroying others. That is to say, legalistic people continually compare themselves with others in order to maintain their splendor.

A man, for example, may believe he's spiritual because he doesn't own a television or a computer. Perhaps he has made that choice to help resist the temptation to view immoral material. That method may be fine for him, but unconsciously he begins to believe that anyone who watches television or uses a computer must be a worldly Christian. As a result, his personal spiritual standard becomes a law by which he judges—and condemns—all others.

Many of us have been legalists at one time or another. I know I was. I walked in my own strength because I was taught to walk in my own strength. I was taught that I was not to do certain things even though the Bible never mentioned them—and people constantly watched me to make sure I followed the rules.

I have since discovered, however, that legalism is a total misunderstanding of the covenant of grace. The covenant of grace doesn't say, "Don't do this or don't do that." The covenant of grace doesn't overwhelm people with man-made spirituality. Instead, the covenant of grace says the risen Christ dwells within us and *He* will do this or do that if we allow Him to work through us.

When people who have been living in their own glory and splendor reach the end of their rope, they can do one of two things. Either they can become cynical and fall into great unbelief, or they can give up trying to create their own glory and begin to walk in the Spirit. People in this second category soon learn that the attention-getting glory of legalism is attractive, but the glory of walking in the Spirit far exceeds it.

Whenever I consider the contrast between the glory of legalism and the glory of the Spirit, I think of Moses. When he was about forty years old, Moses gave up his position and social standing in the royal family of Egypt so he could identify with the sufferings of his people—the Children of Israel. That was a big commitment for him to make. However, Moses thought he could be the man God wanted him to be through sheer personal force. As a result of his sincerity and fervor, he killed an Egyptian. Moses had the right calling, but he tried to conquer the world by hammering it out on his own. That's what legalism does.

Later in life, after meeting God in the burning bush, Moses became a different person. He lived in the glory and splendor of God and through His power led more than a million and a half people out of Egypt to the Promised Land. Had he tried to fulfill God's commission by relying on his own knowledge, Moses would have faced utter failure.

Legalism and Spirit-filled living are mutually exclusive: it is impossible to be both a legalist and a Spirit-filled person. Legalism brings death; the risen Christ brings life. Legalism is written on stone and is concerned with the material realm; the covenant of grace is written on people's hearts and is concerned with the reality of the soul. Legalism has a glory that fades; the glory of grace can never fade.

STOP HIDING BEHIND A VEIL

When we choose to live for God on the basis of our own energy and our own set of spiritual rules, we will discover enormous weaknesses and inadequacies within ourselves. *If others see those weaknesses*, we think, *we'll lose our glory.* So we cover ourselves with a "veil"—a spiritual mask—to preserve that fading glory.

Paul addresses this problem, using the example of Moses:

> Therefore, since we have such a hope, we are very bold. We are not like Moses, who would put a veil over his face to keep the Israelites from gazing at it while the radiance was fading away. But their minds were made dull, for to this day the same veil remains when the old covenant is read. It has not been removed, because only in Christ is it taken away. Even to this day when Moses is read, a veil covers their hearts. But whenever anyone turns to the Lord, the veil is taken away. Now the Lord is the Spirit, and where the Spirit of the Lord is, there is freedom. And we, who with unveiled faces all reflect the Lord's glory, are being transformed into his likeness with ever-increasing glory, which comes from the Lord, who is the Spirit (2 Cor. 3:12–18).

An interesting thing happened to Moses when he received the Ten Commandments in the Lord's presence on Mount Sinai. The experience was so glorious that Moses' face began to shine. When he came back down the mountain to the Israelites, they were afraid of him because his face shone like the sun. But soon the glory began to fade, and Moses did something strange. He covered his face with a veil.

In that culture, only women wore veils. Can you imagine what it was like for Moses—the leader of the Israelites, the man chosen by God to receive the Law—to put on a veil, just like a woman? Imagine how desperate he must have been to think that it was better to hide behind a veil than to allow people to see that the glory of the Law (note 2 Cor. 3:13–15) [Note: the glory was from Moses' being in the presence of God (Ex. 34:29), not from the "Law"]was fading away.

When men and women who have tried to serve God through legalism see that their inner inconsistencies and uncontrolled passions still exist, they begin to cover up. They realize how little glory they have in their own power. So they put on a veil. They carefully create a mask to show the world how spiritual they are, but inside they are miserable. They feel so low that Scripture loses its precious, uplifting meaning. They begin to doubt their beliefs and start an endless search for religious experiences to boost them up, never realizing that their hypocrisy—their protective veil—is destroying them.

Paul's message is that when we live in the power of the indwelling Christ, we don't have to be like Moses. We don't have to cower behind a veil. We don't have to *pretend* that Christ lives in us because He *does* live in us. We don't have to put on a pretty, spiritual-looking covering. When we live honestly and transparently in the indwelling glory of Christ, without a veil to hide behind, people will see our weaknesses. But they also will see beyond our weaknesses and witness the reality of Christ in our lives.

Look again at verse 17: "Now the Lord is the Spirit, and where the Spirit of the Lord is, there is freedom." What a joy! Christians living in the Spirit don't have to be imprisoned by legalistic masks. Not only do we have freedom when we take off our veils, but verse 18 indicates that we will be transformed into Christ's likeness! We will grow steadily into the image of Jesus Christ—if only we stop pretending!

Once, when I spoke on this section of 2 Corinthians, a minister talked with me afterward. "Luis," he said thoughtfully, "I'm forty-three years old and for the first time in my life I'm taking off the mask. In seminary I was trained to put on masks—greet people this way, don't talk too much to these people, don't do this or that—and I've been putting on a show ever since. I'm sick of the show. I'm going to take off the mask and be myself in Christ."

Of course it isn't easy to remove our masks. It took radical surgery for me. I was a pious, self-sufficient legalist, relying on my education and Bible knowledge instead of God. I wore a good-looking, tough mask on the outside, yet I was empty inside. But thanks be to God, He saw through my mask and ripped it off. He saved me from being a proud, legalistic, spiritual casualty.

Paul also points out that struggling to maintain our fading glory isn't the only product of legalism. As long as we persist in wearing our legalistic masks, we cannot truly see the Lord. Our veils not only hide our weaknesses from others, but also come between us and the Lord. The veils harden our minds and hearts, preventing spiritual growth. That's one reason some of us aren't as spiritually mature as we ought to be. Only Christ can take away our veils. We are incapable of removing them ourselves.

In human terms, spiritual growth seems like a contradiction. We tend to think that when we work harder, we make more progress. But the truth is, we can't begin to make progress until we stop working in our own power and allow Christ to work through us. This is no instant makeover. It is a continual process as we reflect "the Lord's glory," not our own. Gradually, we "are being transformed into his (Jesus Christ's) likeness"— not through our own efforts, but through His Spirit.

MINISTERING IN CANDOR

Finally, an open sincerity permeates the ministry of a Christian who walks in the Spirit. Paul outlines the results of sincere, Spirit-filled living in the following passage:

> Therefore, since through God's mercy we have this ministry, we do not lose heart. Rather, we have renounced secret and shameful ways; we do not use deception, nor do we distort the word of God. On the contrary, by setting forth the truth plainly we commend ourselves to every man's conscience in the sight of God. And even if our gospel is veiled, it is veiled to those who are perishing. The god of this age has blinded the minds of unbelievers, so that they cannot see the light of the gospel of the glory of Christ, who is the image of God. For we do not preach ourselves, but Jesus Christ as Lord, and ourselves as your servants for Jesus' sake. For God, who said, "Let light shine out of darkness," made his light shine in our hearts to give us the light of the knowledge of the glory of God in the face of Christ (2 Cor. 4:1–6).

When we minister the life of Christ, we don't lose heart. If we really believe everything Paul says in this passage (and if we don't, we're just fooling ourselves), God will encourage us. In effect, Paul is saying, "Hey, Christ indwells you. You have adequacy. You have glory. You don't have to hide behind a veil to keep people from seeing you as you are. Therefore, don't lose heart." That is the first consequence of living in open sincerity through the Holy Spirit.

I think Paul had a very good reason for reminding us not to lose heart in God's ministry. After all, our weaknesses show when we take off our masks. We feel weak and vulnerable. We have admitted to the world that we aren't everything people would like us to be. We may face the strong temptation to go back to our protective façades. But remember: don't lose heart! Don't go back to an old way of living when the future promises so much.

The second consequence of living in open sincerity of the indwelling Christ is that we are not disgraceful or underhanded; we do not tamper with God's Word. That means we honestly and sincerely proclaim God's truth, and do not use Scripture to gain our own ends.

We must be careful when we claim to speak honestly. Some people have a tendency to offend almost everyone; when approached about their lack of sensitivity they reply, "Well, I'm a very honest person. I always speak the truth." What they really are saying is, "I love to rip off other people's masks, but don't touch mine. I like it just the way it is."

This is not the kind of sincerity Paul is talking about! Christians are responsible for taking off their own masks—not anyone else's. Although we can encourage and counsel others to become authentic in their Christian lives, change results from the power of God and each individual's willingness to walk in His light.

Living in sincerity and authenticity also means that we refuse to stoop to sneaky or devious ways of ministry. We don't slander or malign Christian coworkers. We don't take unethical tax breaks. In short, we refuse to use our own methods to accomplish God's work.

Jacob is a notable example of a deceitful, underhanded person. Jacob had a great future before him. God had selected him to rule his brother, and he knew it. Yet he refused to wait for God to do what He had promised. Instead, Jacob devised a scheme whereby he could cheat his brother and deceive his father. He created such turmoil in his family that he had to flee.

Eventually, Jacob tried to make a deal with God. When he was in the wilderness, he begged God for safety and prosperity, promising to return to God one tenth of everything He would give him. The audacity of Jacob! Was he expecting God to drool over his offer?

Before we condemn Jacob, though, we should remember one thing: we can be just like him. When we're caught violating a trust or being poor stewards of our ministry, don't we usually try to make deals with God too?

In contrast, consider Joseph's life. Although he was a son of the deceitful Jacob, Joseph walked in open sincerity. He was not devious, cunning, or sneaky. He always was honest and upright before God and man. At times his honesty was costly. His refusal to accept the immoral offer of Potiphar's wife landed him in jail. Yet Joseph walked in God's light and never lost heart. Because of his faithfulness, God richly blessed Joseph throughout his life and many others received God's blessing through him. That's the way to walk in God's light. That's authentic, powerful Christian living!

Today we need to stop pretending. People need to see Christ in us, but they will never see Him as long as we cover up our failures and *pretend* to be Spirit-filled Christians. Near our ministry's international headquarters in Portland, Oregon, there is a sign for a church that claims to be a "Spirit-filled Fellowship." That sign can only be true—and I do hope that it is—when a church is populated with Spirit-filled individuals. We are not Spirit-filled because the sign outside says so. It is when we give up our masks, our own version of righteousness, and depend solely on the power of the Holy Spirit that the fragrance of Christ will come through. People will see our authenticity, and through us they will see Christ!

This message is no less important today than it was when Paul first explained it. In fact, it may even be more important today because we are in the midst of a great spiritual harvest. It is imperative that we grasp the moment and make the most of the opportunities God has given us.

As columnist Art Buchwald says, "Whether these are the best of times or the worst of times, it's the only time we've got." We have only one lifetime—our generation—in which to serve Christ. We are not responsible for what has or has not happened in previous generations. We are not responsible for future generations; we can do little for them except leave a legacy that honors the Lord. But we are fully responsible for the mark we leave on our generation.

We now have unprecedented opportunities to proclaim the Gospel. Sure, we see the continuing influence of New Age and Eastern religions and a disregard for godliness and human life. Around the globe, our brothers and sisters in Christ endure rising persecution and martyrdom for their faith. Even in America, we are not immune to terror. But we still have greater freedom and more available technology to proclaim the Gospel than any generation before us. And where once we saw only doors locked against the Good News, God has given unprecedented open doors.

Who would have thought that, when this book was first published in 1985, we would soon be preaching the Gospel behind what was known as the Iron Curtain of the Soviet communist regime? In 1989 I was invited to preach the Gospel in the Soviet Union, including the Olympic stadium in Leningrad. Then, in May 1990 I preached in stadiums in three cities in Romania—just days after the first free elections in that nation. We have been back to the struggling countries of Eastern Europe many times since.

In 1999, I had the privilege of partnering with other evangelists in saturating the small country of Latvia with the Gospel. On the opening night of the Hope '99 crusade, Lativa's former president Guntis Ulmanis urged the audience and, via television, the nation to listen carefully to our message of hope. Then, on the last day of the crusade, I preached in the historic Dome Cathedral in the capital of Riga. That evening, Mr. Ulmanis himself came forward to make a public commitment to Jesus Christ. Two years later, he sent me his greetings as a brother continuing to grow in his spiritual walk.

When I was a child, China intrigued me. I listened to my mother read the story of Hudson Taylor, the founder of China Inland Mission (OMF International), and I longed to preach the Gospel in Shanghai, just as Taylor did. For years, the door to Western missionaries has been tightly shut, but the Spirit of God has been at work among the Chinese people. Then, in 1997, the churches of Hong Kong invited our evangelistic team for a crusade. Watching a video of the crusade later on, I was surprised to hear myself saying to the new believers, "I'll either see you in heaven or I'll see you in Shanghai!" I didn't even remember saying it, but God made it come true. Three years later, the Lord opened the way for me to preach evangelistic messages in three churches in Shanghai, as well as address students at East China Theological Seminary and Fudan University.

As I dialogued with Chinese officials at the Religious Affairs Bureau, one man noted that I liked big stadiums and big crowds. I shared with him my dream of coming back to Shanghai and preaching in massive Shanghai Stadium. Better yet, I pray God will open the parks to a festival that will reach more of the city's fourteen million people. Will God answer that prayer soon? We don't know the timetable. In the meantime, our evangelistic team has prepared a Chinese website to be accessed by more Chinese people than could ever fit in one stadium or park.

Many are still blinded by the god of this world. But many in the midst of our generation are listening intently to the Gospel of Christ. God is removing the veil and letting the light of the Gospel shine in their hearts.

In the United States, Christians are exerting an increasing influence on government and society. Even as cynicism toward Christians seems prevalent, the testimonies of people of faith cannot be suppressed. The Gospel is preached in the stories that cross our headlines.

Back in 1999, we launched the first of our new-styled evangelistic festivals in the United States in my hometown of Portland, Oregon. I told a reporter with *The Oregonian*, "If 10,000 people come, I'll be very happy. If 50,000 come, I'll be out of my mind." That first night, as I looked out over a crowd of 38,000 people—and then 55,000 people the second night—I was delirious with joy. God continues to bring more people to our festivals than we ever dreamed of before.

I have made it a point to accept invitations from the White House no matter who currently presides in office. As Christians, the Bible calls us to pray for our president and those in leadership. Within days of the terrorist attacks on Washington and New York, I was invited to the White House with other religious leaders. President Bush urged us to call our people to pray for our nation. Then he went on to give a clear testimony of his faith in Jesus Christ.

In the months that followed, I twice had the privilege of leading the White House staff Bible study.

But it isn't just on top political levels that God is working. After September 11, 2001, people flocked back to church. The Sunday following the tragedy, 28 million people came to church who had not attended before. Unfortunately, by January 2002, only 4 million of those new attenders remained in church as the sense of spiritual urgency waned. Still, for those who came to church and heard the message of Jesus Christ, their lives will never be the same.

Mike was one of those people. When the President proclaimed September 14, 2001, a national day of prayer, Mike wanted to participate. He approached his Christian neighbors and asked about going to a prayer service. Damon and Elise gladly took Mike and his wife to church for the service—and continued to share the Good News in a clear manner. The light of the Gospel shone in Mike's heart and he committed his life to Jesus Christ.

Every day, our indelible influence—whether for good or ill—affects every person we meet and every task we undertake. One of Paul's purposes in this portion of 2 Corinthians is to make us aware of our influence and encourage us to live as Christians—as men and women God has sent to minister to the world around us.

FOR PERSONAL REFLECTION

Read 2 Corinthians 3:1–18

1. "Some of us have fallen into the trap of pretending to be Christians. We act pious, victorious. and radiant because that is what others expect of us." Can you recall a time when you were just putting on a Christian façade? What pressures do you feel to live according to other people's expectations? What does God expect from you instead?

2. "Most of us are painfully aware of our failings. . . . Just as we are conscious of our own inadequacy, we must be conscious of the competence God has given us." What failures and inadequacies seem to hinder you most? How can God make you competent in spite of these struggles?

3. "The glory of legalism also fades away because there is a limit to a legalistic person's strength." Have you ever tried a legalistic approach to living victoriously in Christ? How long did it last? Why is God's way of grace both more permanent and more glorious than the ministry of the law?

4. "When we live honestly and transparently in the indwelling of Christ, without a veil to hide behind, people will see our weaknesses." Which weaknesses are you trying to hide from others? How might others see the reality of Christ more clearly when you live transparently?

5. "We are not responsible for future generations. . . . But we are fully responsible for the mark we leave on our generation." What mark will you leave on your generation?

FOR INTERACTIVE DISCUSSION

Read aloud 2 Corinthians 3:1–4:6

1. "Either we have handwritten approval from man, or divine approval from the Spirit." What is it about us that proves to others that our lives and our ministries are genuine?

2. "God delivers us from our own inadequacy, granting us tremendous confidence through the Holy Spirit to minister life to others." What is the difference between making a positive impact and ministering life to others? How does the Holy Spirit use us to do this?

3. "You have to admit that legalistic people seem to have a certain amount of glorious splendor." Why do legalistic people sometimes seem to have it all together? What could be driving a legalistic approach to spiritual growth and victory?

4. "In human terms, spiritual growth seems like a contradiction." Why are we incapable of making progress on our own? How does spiritual growth actually happen?

5. "Finally, an open sincerity permeates the ministry of a Christian who walks in the Spirit." What does it mean to live in open sincerity? What are the consequences—both painful and wonderful —of living this way?

CHAPTER 8

Experiencing Inner Renewal

If you were to consider the desires, motives, thoughts, and actions of most Christians, I think you would discover that every growing believer basically wants the same thing. New or mature, young or old, charismatic or noncharismatic, every Christian desires to live a fulfilling life in the presence of God. Every Christian longs to communicate Christ in a powerful way. And every Christian seeks spiritual renewal on a daily basis.

As Christians, we absolutely detest any hint of stagnation in our spiritual lives. We want to feel that we're growing, changing, and developing spiritually. We long for reality in our walk with God. We don't want to feel that we're stuck in the same place we were at five years ago. We long to have new, joyous experiences in the Lord—and that longing comes from the Holy Spirit.

But so often we pursue renewal in the wrong ways. When we don't feel a sense of daily renewal, we run from church to church, pastor to pastor, denomination to denomination, experience to experience, looking for renewal. We even have "renewal congresses." In fact, I've received advertisements for renewal congresses in the Holy Land. I guess people think that if they can walk where Jesus walked, they'll be renewed.

People also have talked to me about "renewal" in their churches.

"Oh," they say, "our minister doesn't preach from the pulpit anymore. He wears a wireless mike and talks while he walks among the congregation. And we don't sit in rows anymore. We sit together in a big circle. It's wonderful."

If that's all spiritual renewal is, then my family experiences a renewal every spring when my wife moves the living room furniture around. I like to keep things the same way, but Pat just loves to change them. I like my reading chair to be in a familiar spot. I don't care whether it fits in with the surroundings or color coordinates. I don't care about the carpeting or the plants around it. But Pat loves renewal, and every spring our house is renewed.

Moving church furniture around—or even moving church programs around—may symbolize renewal, but it certainly isn't what spiritual renewal is all about. Some people believe that a lot of noise and outward change means renewal. These outward signs sometimes indicate renewal, but more often than not they're just another type of mask or religious façade.

The kind of daily renewal we desperately long for as Christians cannot be found in a uniquely shaped building, in a different furniture arrangement, or in a more creative form of worship. The spiritual renewal we seek must come from the life of Jesus working in us and flowing through us day after day. Spiritual renewal is the evidence of Christ's work in our lives.

WE HAVE THE LIFE OF JESUS WITHIN US

If the spiritual renewal we long for is a result of the life of Jesus at work within us, how can this life be appropriated? The answer is found in the following verses:

> But we have this treasure in jars of clay to show that this all-surpassing power is from God and not from us. We are hard pressed on every side, but not crushed; perplexed, but not in despair; persecuted, but not abandoned; struck down, but not destroyed. We always carry around in our body the death of Jesus, so that the life of Jesus may also be revealed in our body. For we who are alive are always being given over to death for Jesus' sake, so that his life may be revealed in our mortal body. So then, death is at work in us, but life is at work in you (2 Cor. 4:7–12).

In the first verse of this passage you will notice that we, as Christians, have a treasure within us. This treasure is nothing less than God Himself! No matter who we are—grandfathers, students, factory workers, home-makers, business executives—no matter what we look like—skinny, chub-by, tall, short—God has come to indwell us, making our bodies temples of the Holy Spirit.

This truth—that the living God lives within us—is the heart of the Gospel. Of course Jesus' death on the cross and His resurrection are the foundation of the Gospel, but the heart of the Gospel is that God Himself *indwells* us. God isn't out there in orbit with the satellites. He is within us. The Bible says that when we are joined to the Lord, we become one spir-it with Him (1 Cor. 6:17). Spiritual renewal, then, is the result of the cru-cified and resurrected Christ living within each one of us.

Paul mentions that this marvelous treasure is contained in earthen ves-sels. The earthen vessels he refers to are our human bodies. The Bible says that our bodies were made from the earth. When we die, our bodies go back into the earth and disintegrate to become part of nature once again. Yet God has chosen to dwell within our humble, temporal, imperfect human bodies.

Our earthen vessels are fragile; we have to treat them with great care. We feed them, wash them, clothe them, protect them. And if we neglect our bodies for even a few days, they begin to show our earthly beginnings all too quickly!

Several years ago I realized just how fragile our human bodies are. I noticed five spots on my face and asked a dermatologist to look at them. He examined them and said, "Well, these are precancerous. We'd better burn them off." So he burned them off and that was the end of the prob-lem. But then I started thinking. Today I had spots burned off. Tomorrow, some other part of me will need attention. Even though I jog and exer-cise regularly and try to eat nutritious food, my body really isn't such a great piece of equipment. No matter how hard I work to keep my pot of clay in shape, one day it *will* fall apart. But the beautiful thing is that no mat-ter how unimpressive our earthly, human bodies are, God has chosen to be the treasure within us. In our bodies dwell the power and the glory of the resurrected Christ.

Many believers accept this concept intellectually, but live their lives as though God were up in heaven somewhere. They hustle around here on earth trying to do their best for God, never realizing that Christ actually lives within them. They never come to grips with the reality that the eternal, living God has chosen to live within and to work through every believer. What an awesome thought! What a difference that treasure makes in a person's life!

It's easy to forget that even though it is glorious to be a Christian and to have the great treasure of Christ living within us, we are not exempt from the troubles of life. Paul clearly states that the treasure of the indwelling Christ doesn't eliminate every problem (2 Cor. 4:8–9). He says that we are afflicted, perplexed, persecuted, and struck down—just like the unbelievers around us. But we can respond to these daily problems differently because Christ is within us!

Christians are afflicted just like everyone else. People cheat us. People say bad things about us. Our cars break down. Our children get sick. Friends and family members die. We have the same kinds of problems our unbelieving neighbors have, but we are not crushed by affliction because Christ lives within us.

The fact that we are not crushed by the afflictions of daily life is a distinguishing mark of the Christian. We may look just like unbelievers from the outside, but inside we have the blessing of the indwelling Christ to carry us through all affliction.

Sometimes we're perplexed and confused by life. Our friends may turn against us. We may be unable to resolve a problem at work, home, or church. Things may happen to us that we don't understand, but we are not driven to despair because Christ lives within us.

We are persecuted, too. We may not face ongoing, physical persecution for the sake of Christ, as our brothers and sisters do in many countries. But even in America, Christian students are gunned down for their faith, and churches are bombed for their witness. At some time or another, we all face social persecution. We may become good friends with our neighbors, but when we begin to share the Good News with them, they may not invite us to their parties anymore. But persecution isn't the end of the world. And dying for Christ is not the end of life—it is a glorious entrance into eternity with God. No matter who turns against us in life, we never will be forsaken by the indwelling Christ.

Finally, Paul says we will be struck down, but never destroyed. I suppose I shouldn't admit it, but I like to watch boxing. It reminds me of spiritual warfare. When a guy takes a hard punch and reels to the floor, you may think he's been knocked out and the match is over. But then he gets up and starts throwing punches again. That's the kind of spiritual picture Paul describes here. As Christians, we may be knocked down, but the indwelling Christ enables us to get up and go again.

WHAT IT MEANS TO CARRY THE DEATH OF JESUS WITHIN US

If the power of the living Christ is in every believer, why isn't it always visible? Why do we sometimes feel a sense of defeat, depression, frustration, and fruitlessness?

Paul explains the reason for the defeat that cripples so many Christians by stating, "We always carry around in our body the death of Jesus, so that the life of Jesus may also be revealed in our body" (2 Cor. 4:10). This verse indicates that the *death* of Jesus must be at work in us before we can see the results of the *life* of Christ. But how does the death of Jesus work in us? What does it mean in our daily lives?

It took me a long time to really understand this passage. I had decided, as every Christian must, to follow the admonition "to offer your bodies as living sacrifices, holy and pleasing to God—this is your spiritual act of worship" (Rom. 12:1). That decision was crucial. I had prayed, "I don't want to be a worldly Christian. Lord Jesus, here is my whole body, soul, and spirit. I dedicate them to You." But like so many others, I assumed that choosing to commit myself to Christ was a one-time decision.

Two cross-references to this passage bewildered me for a long time. In John 12:24, Jesus speaks of the grain of wheat that must fall to the ground and die before it can bear fruit. Then again in Matthew 16:24 Jesus says that anyone who does not take up his cross and follow Him cannot be His disciple. I was stumped.

No matter how many times I heard preachers speak about the grain of wheat, I didn't understand it. I didn't know how to make a hole in the ground, fall into it, and die for the Lord so I could bear fruit. And I didn't know what Jesus meant by taking up the cross.

Through further study, I have come to believe that these three passages mean basically the same thing. That is, every time my will conflicts with God's will, and I choose His over mine, the death of Jesus is at work in me. When I choose God's will over and against my will, the grain of wheat falls to the ground and dies so that it can bear fruit. When I choose God's will over my will, I am taking up the cross of Jesus.

These passages don't deal with the initial decision that an individual makes to follow Christ, but with the future decisions every Christian must make in order to walk with the living Christ. Making that first decision to follow Christ only lays the foundation for a lifetime of daily decisions to follow Christ.

Commitment, then, isn't something we do once and never have to settle again. Commitment doesn't permanently eliminate conflict within our souls. We must continue to choose God's will over ours. But when we do so, the Lord Jesus—who indwells us by the Holy Spirit—will work through us in dynamic ways.

In the Garden of Gethsemane, Jesus provided a perfect example of someone who chose God's will over human will. Jesus was the perfect man. He knew God's will for His life and wanted it. Nevertheless, as a man, Jesus didn't want to be crucified. He wasn't a masochist who couldn't wait to be beaten and mocked, who couldn't wait for the nails to be pounded through His hands. He knew the emotional and spiritual agony He would suffer as the guilt of the world was placed upon Him and His own Father turned away. Jesus prayed that He wouldn't have to drink such a bitter cup. But Jesus knew the will of the Father and chose God's will over His own—not in resignation, but in a clear-cut, meaningful decision.

Jesus' choice is an example to all of us. Whenever we choose God's will over ours, the death of Jesus is at work in us. We are dying to ego, pride, passion, and our own desires. When we choose God's will over our own, we become Christ-conscious instead of self-conscious, and the life of Jesus begins to flow through us. God then can use us to bring life to others because He is having His way in our lives.

In my life, I often must choose God's will over my own. As an evangelist, one of the most difficult choices I had to make—and I had to make it repeatedly—was to leave my wife and four sons at home and go off to preach the Gospel at a crusade or conference. It was a real battle. Many times I would rather stay at home. Yet I knew I must make the right choice. When I chose God's will over my will, I knew that the death of Jesus would be at work in me and the life of Jesus would be flowing through me. I knew that God was going to use me to do something for His glory because He was having His way in my life.

At the same time, I also made a choice that, when I was with my family, I would truly be with them. For me, that meant my free time wasn't spent on the green playing golf. I have nothing against the game of golf, but choosing God's will for me as a father meant giving up some of "my" free time to be with my family.

With my sons now grown up and married, I now have the freedom to travel for months at a time, and Pat is free to come with me on many of these trips. Plus, God has given me the incredible privilege of serving Him alongside three of my sons who are members of our evangelistic association. Our youngest son, Stephen, is an active member of our home church and a strong witness for Jesus Christ as a public school teacher. The things I "gave up" for God seemed like small deaths years ago—but God has brought great life from them.

My former team member and now partner evangelist Dan Owens tells a similar story. In 1997, Dan was invited to speak at an evangelistic campaign in Lahore, Pakistan. Normally, he would jump at the chance to preach anywhere, but this situation was a little different. This time Dan would be leaving not just his wife and two teenage boys, but a newborn son, too. This time he would be traveling as an American Christian into a Muslim country and speaking at a stadium named for Mu'ammar al-Gadhafi, Libya's enigmatic leader.

Dan was experiencing real fears over this trip, so he decided to phone Brother Andrew of Open Doors—a man who had spent years making trips into communist Eastern Europe to deliver Bibles to Christians who risked imprisonment to own a copy of God's Word. Brother Andrew advised him to go—not as an opportunity for Dan, but as an opportunity for the Gospel.

Dan did go to Pakistan for eight days. While he was there, members of the committee organizing the campaign received death threats. The day before he arrived, a truck full of men with machine guns parked outside the chairman of the committee's home and pointed their guns at the house. Minutes before Dan walked onto the platform, one of the men assigned as a bodyguard told him, "If you say the wrong thing tonight, our enemies are here, and they will kill you on the spot."

Even without being physically harmed, Dan was experiencing the death of Jesus as he preached in that volatile situation. But he experienced the incredible joy of seeing life come to hundreds of people that week. He chose God's will over his own—and he was rewarded.

Most of the time, we don't have to make choices about moving overseas or going into dangerous situations to follow God's will. Our choices are as mundane as words we speak about a friend or coworker, or fulfilling a commitment we've made at work or church. Our choices revolve around possessions and schedules and attitudes.

So we may think the choices we have to make between our will and God's will are insignificant and of little importance. We think, *Oh, this decision isn't important. It won't matter if I choose my will instead of God's this time.* But that is not the case. Every time we choose God's will over our own, the life of Jesus flows through us. When we choose our will instead of God's, we are refusing the death of Jesus. We are refusing to carry the cross. We are refusing to die like a grain of wheat so that we may bear fruit. We miss the blessing of the life of Jesus flowing through us and cause others to miss that blessing too.

Several years ago I had the opportunity to share the Gospel with the president of the Dominican Republic. Our evangelistic team was in Santo Domingo for a crusade and we held a leadership breakfast. The president did not attend, but sent a lawyer to represent him. As I spoke with her, she said, "The president would like to meet you before you leave the country. But he can see you only on Sunday, immediately after Mass, in the chapel of the presidential palace. If you come to Mass with him, he will have forty-five minutes to talk with you. His chauffeur will pick you up at 8:30 Sunday morning."

"I'll be there!" I said. As far as I knew, no one had ever witnessed to this man before. What an exciting opportunity!

But then I began to worry. *Some non-Catholic Christians might hear about me sitting through Mass and will become upset with me,* I thought. *I can't go through with this.* I talked with some pastors in Santo Domingo who confirmed my fear. They told me I'd better not go. Then I consulted a Christian lawyer who worked closely with the government; he told me I should go to Mass and witness to the president. I knew what the Lord would have me do—but I turned coward. When the chauffeur arrived, I sent him away.

Was I ever discouraged afterward! My joy was gone. That afternoon, I prayed, "Lord, forgive me. I'll never turn down an opportunity to witness to somebody because I fear what others might think." The Lord gave me forgiveness and relief about this incident, but I learned in a very real way that the life of Jesus cannot flow through me to others if I choose my will over His.

Older Christians sometimes face a danger in this area. They may suddenly stop choosing God's will over their own. They may think, as David did when he committed immorality with Bathsheba, *Hey, I've been serving the Lord faithfully for more than twenty years. It's time for me to take it easy for a while. It's not going to hurt to do things my way.* But living for Christ is not something we decide to do just for a specified period of time. We must continuously decide to choose God's will over our own.

Whenever we knowingly refuse God's will, we experience defeat, discouragement, and depression. We cannot be filled with the joy of the Spirit. We miss out on the opportunities and blessings God wants to bestow upon us. But if we confess our sins—if we confess the times we have chosen our will rather than God's—He will cleanse, purify, and use us.

THE LIFE OF JESUS AND SHARING WITH OTHERS

One characteristic of believers who walk with the indwelling Christ is that they find ways to share their knowledge of Christ. They don't have to be kicked, shoved, pushed, or cajoled into witnessing. They don't have to be harangued by a minister or carry on in grim determination. A believer who is filled with the indwelling life of Christ will find ways to share the Gospel according to his or her temperament, talents, education, and position in life—not in a pushy, overbearing way, but naturally, under the Holy Spirit's guidance.

Paul describes this phenomenon:

> It is written: "I believed; therefore I have spoken." With that same spirit of faith we also believe and therefore speak, because we know that the one who raised the Lord Jesus from the dead will also raise us with Jesus and present us with you in his presence. All this is for your benefit, so that the grace that is reaching more and more people may cause thanksgiving to overflow to the glory of God (2 Cor. 4:13–15).

See? We speak because we believe. We don't speak because we're brilliant. We don't speak because someone told us to. We don't speak to alleviate our guilt. We speak because we believe. We're so excited about what we've found in Christ that we want to share it with others. We speak because God makes us capable of loving others and sharing the Good News with them.

God can use any human being for His glory—no matter how little ability, charisma, or knowledge that person may seem to possess. Ordinary people have spoken naturally out of their belief and God has used them to open up whole countries to the Gospel. One of these people is my friend Dave Farah, a Wycliffe missionary to Bolivia.

Like many Wycliffe workers, Dave is dedicated to serving the Lord and is a powerful witness for Christ. In 1964, after working as an administrator at Wycliffe's Jungle Center in Bolivia for eight years, he was asked to move to La Paz, the capital city, to take over the responsibility of government relations.

Shortly after moving to La Paz, Dave contacted the minister of education, a military colonel. Dave started to pray for this man, asking the Lord for an opportunity to witness to him. Before long, however, a revolution took place and the colonel disappeared. Revolutions are nothing new in South America. Bolivia has averaged more than one revolution a year for the past 160 years. But Dave had a bad feeling about the colonel's disappearance. No one seemed to know where he was. So Dave prayed for an opportunity to help him.

One day a newspaper reported that the colonel had sought refuge in the Argentinean embassy. When Dave learned of this, he prayed for a way to contact the colonel. He wanted to try to get a New Testament to him. Dave underlined verses in the Spanish New Testament, enclosed a letter explaining the way of salvation, and gave it to the guard at the Argentinean embassy, asking him to give it to the colonel. Dave walked away, not knowing whether his request would be honored.

Later, the colonel telephoned Dave—an American missionary, a foreigner—and said, "You were the only person who contacted me while I was in hiding. My friends ignored me. I had nothing else to do, so I read the New Testament."

Soon another revolution took place and the colonel became president of Bolivia. Shortly after the inauguration, Dave telephoned the colonel and asked to see him. The colonel immediately set up an appointment, greeted Dave like an old friend, and gave him a big hug (as we Latins do).

"What can I do for you?" the colonel asked, expecting Dave to ask a favor.

"Nothing," Dave replied. "I just want to pray for you, your family, your government, and Bolivia."

"No one has ever prayed for me before," the colonel said, shaking his head in amazement. "Please, pray for me."

So Dave prayed. When he finished, the colonel was crying. He was so thankful that Dave had prayed for him.

Before long, Dave invited the colonel to accompany him on a vacation. "Wycliffe has a house in the jungle where it's nice and warm. Let's go down there to relax and enjoy some fishing."

During their vacation, Dave and the colonel talked about many things, including corruption and lack of trust in the government. Dave suggested that the country needed a moral revival, and the colonel became excited about the idea. In fact, he asked Dave to draw up a plan for a morality campaign in Bolivia!

Part of the plan included Bolivia's first presidential prayer breakfast, at which I was invited to speak. During this breakfast I had an intimate conversation with the colonel. He opened his heart and shared his deepest concerns with me. Here was a man who had the same personal and family problems all the rest of us had, plus the worries of governing more than six million people. As we talked, I was able to explain God's plan of salvation to him. It took him awhile to believe that God would forgive him for some of the things he had done, but before we parted he received Christ as his Savior.

Grateful for his new relationship with Christ, the colonel asked, "Palau, what can I do for you while you're in Bolivia?"

"Well," I replied, "our crusade is scheduled to run for five days. It would be fantastic if we could be on national television during that time."

The colonel immediately told an aide to put our program on the national network for five nights. "What time would be best for you?" he asked.

"Ten to eleven in the evening," I said.

"Fine. You have five nights from ten to eleven."

What an exciting opportunity! But there's more. We received three thousand *Living New Testaments* from the World Home Bible League to offer free during the television program. We gave all three thousand away.

When the colonel saw that we were giving New Testaments to the people, he decided that all the religious education classes in Bolivia should be based on the New Testament. With the help of the World Home Bible

League, Dave offered the government a million copies of the *Living New Testament*. They since have been used in religious education classes throughout Bolivia and played a significant role in the spiritual awakening of that country!

Dave wanted only to help translate the New Testament, but he had an impact on an entire nation that continues to this day! This great work was not the result of a single, momentous decision, but of one man continuously obeying God in little things—praying for a military officer, sending a New Testament to someone in need, extending genuine care and friendship to him.

When we walk believing that the life of Jesus is at work within us, we will share the Good News with others. We may stumble along the way, we may make mistakes, but we will communicate. Sometimes we make the mistake of thinking, *If I were better looking, I could be a great soul winner. If I were a more dynamic speaker, people would listen to me.* But that's not the point. The secret is not in what we look like from the outside, but in the treasure at work within us whenever we choose God's will over our own.

LIVING IN DAILY RENEWAL

The power of the indwelling Christ is what keeps dynamic Christians alive and excited about life. Persistence is the preeminent characteristic of God's outstanding servants throughout church history. John Wesley, who God used to bring revival to England and the young colonies in America, and Corrie ten Boom, who endured a concentration camp for protecting Jews during World War II and set up recovery homes for survivors afterwards, immediately come to mind. Both were preaching and serving God long after the age most people hope to retire. They didn't keep on out of their own stubbornness, like many unhappy Christians who strive to serve God out of their own ability. Rather, these servants persistently walked in the power of the indwelling Christ. This gave them freedom from worry about their mistakes, problems, and weaknesses.

As we walk in the power of the indwelling Christ, eternity's values become more important to us. Lost people become our obsession because lost people are God's obsession. Although we still hold jobs, earn a living, and pay bills, these things no longer are the focus of our lives. Although we work to keep ourselves attractive, we are not engrossed in clothes, hairstyles, or shoes. Our primary purpose and source of excitement is to reach out to the lost.

I am greatly concerned about the number of Christians today who live unbalanced lives, who seek the excitement and thrills of ego-centered activities. Our greatest kicks in life should not come from the plastic excitement of new cars, houses, or the latest vacation spots. The excitement of seeing the living Christ transform people is the real excitement we should seek. We never can be excited Christians without sharing Jesus Christ.

When the life of Jesus is at work within us, enabling us to communicate the Gospel naturally as we go through life, we will be renewed day by day. Spiritual renewal isn't a movement. It is a daily experience that occurs when we walk in obedience to the indwelling Christ—choosing His will over our own will again and again and again.

One of the exciting things about spiritual renewal is that the older we are and the longer we walk with Christ, the more renewed and youthful we become. As Paul says, "Though outwardly we are wasting away, yet inwardly we are being renewed day by day" (2 Cor. 4:16). What a thrill! When we walk with Christ, our physical bodies may weaken and fall apart, but inside we are growing spiritually stronger every day. Can you imagine how "super-renewed" you will be after choosing God's will over your will for fifty, sixty, or seventy years? Your old body may fall apart, but the inner person is just beginning to show through.

Many people know Bill Bright as the founder of Campus Crusade for Christ and the author of that famous yellow booklet *The Four Spiritual Laws*. Through the influence of his ministry, millions of people have come to Christ. That many and more have been trained to share the Gospel and the Spirit-filled life. You might think that Bill has accomplished his lifework and he can sit back and take it easy until God calls him home.

The fact is that Bill's passion for Jesus Christ and the Gospel has only grown with the years. Back in the early 1970s, Bill would sign his letters, "Yours for fulfilling the Great Commission in 1984." Now he's saying, "Yours for fulfilling the Great Commission in 2010." Even though he's dying of pulmonary fibrosis and needs an oxygen tank to help him breathe, he isn't giving up his dream of reaching the world for Jesus Christ.

When we are renewed through Jesus Christ, the excitement never dies. We don't lose heart! The life of Jesus just flows stronger and stronger, spiritually renewing us more and more. We live authentic, joyful, and victorious lives because the Lord Jesus is alive and working within us. This is what Christianity is all about. It isn't a religion we follow—it's the life of Christ that fills us, making us new people.

FOR PERSONAL REFLECTION

Read 2 Corinthians 4:7–15.

1. "Every Christian desires to live a fulfilling life in the presence of God." What are your longings for your spiritual life? Express those to God right now.

2. "We may look just like unbelievers from the outside, but inside we have the blessing of the indwelling Christ to carry us through all affliction." How is your life just like that of your unbelieving friends and neighbors? How is it different?

3. "Every time my will conflicts with God's will, and I choose His over mine, the death of Jesus is at work in me." Where does your will conflict with God's will? How will you follow through in choosing His will? How can you reveal the death and life of Jesus in your body today?

4. "Lost people become our obsession because lost people are God's obsession." Is this statement true of you? How does focusing on eternal values—and the eternal destiny of those around you— renew you spiritually?

5. "When we walk with Christ, our physical bodies may weaken and fall apart, but inside we are growing spiritually stronger each day." Think over your life so far. How have you seen your inner life grow? Look ahead. What kind of Christian would you like to be when you are nearing life's end? How do you envision being spiritually renewed for the rest of your life?

FOR INTERACTIVE DISCUSSION

Read aloud 2 Corinthians 4:7–15.

1. "So often we pursue renewal in the wrong ways." What are some ineffective—and even detrimental—ways of pursuing spiritual renewal? What is the true source of inner renewal?

2. "This truth—that the living God lives within us—is the heart of the Gospel." Why is the indwelling presence of God the *heart* of the Gospel? What difference does it make knowing that the God of the universe indwells you?

3. Read Matthew 16:24–26 and John 12:24–25. Why is "taking up your cross" and "losing your life" an ongoing process? In what areas of your life have you experienced the continual need to choose God's will over your own?

4. "One characteristic of believers who walk with the indwelling Christ is that they find ways to share their knowledge of Christ." What are your reasons for sharing the Good News of Jesus Christ? How do these reasons either help you or cause you problems? How might God use you—with your unique temperament and even with your weaknesses—to reveal Himself to others?

5. "Spiritual renewal isn't a movement. It is a daily experience that occurs when we walk in obedience to the indwelling Christ." How does daily renewal make a difference in our lives? Think of someone you know who has exhibited this kind of lifelong spiritual renewal. What characterizes his or her life?

CHAPTER 9

Keeping Eternity in View

Human rights, political activism, education, social justice, environmentalism. These are just a few of the causes that have captured the attention and energy of today's people, including many Christians.

All of these causes have their proper place in the lives of believers. But none should ever become an all-consuming passion. It's easy to become so involved in an activity, a cause, or the pursuit of a personal goal that we lose our perspective. Driven by our sincerity and dedication to hard work, we too easily forget that our primary purpose on earth—our all-consuming passion—should be to please God. And we please God by allowing Jesus' love to flow through us so that others will be reconciled to Him.

When our primary aim as Christians is to please God, we can focus our lives on the concerns of God, instead of allowing the world's concerns to distract us. We no longer perceive life in terms of visible, earthly values. Rather, we view life in terms of God's unseen, eternal values. Having this perspective frees us from an overwhelming passion for material possessions. God's eternal perspective enables us to see beyond the hazards of our future here on earth to the certainty of everlasting life with Him. The activities, causes, and goals of our lives become secondary to the goal of pleasing God.

RENEWED CHRISTIANS FOCUS ON ETERNAL VALUES

As renewed Christians, we are not to let our possessions rule us. We may have and appreciate earthly goods, but we are not to be envious—eager to possess more. Although it is fun to have possessions and to buy new ones, we are not to cling to them. This is one of the distinctive characteristics of Christians who experience spiritual renewal on a daily basis. Paul explains why this is true:

> For our light and momentary troubles are achieving for us an eternal glory that far outweighs them all. So we fix our eyes not on what is seen, but on what is unseen. For what is seen is temporary, but what is unseen is eternal (2 Cor. 4:17–18).

The things of this earth pass away quickly; we should, therefore, hold on to them lightly. Yet time and again, we seem to covet material possessions, ignoring the fact that what was valuable one day may be worthless the next. In international finance, for example, a certain currency may be popular at a given time. Other nations are eager to exchange their own money for it. But with changing economic conditions, this same currency—which was valuable only a day before—suddenly may depreciate in value. Then it becomes extremely difficult to trade. Tourists caught holding a worthless currency in a foreign nation will have problems finding a fair exchange rate for their money.

It is sad when men and women in their fifties and sixties are still selfish children at heart—wild, possessed by a passion to buy "one more thing." They have a grim look about them. They think they are mature and have it all together, but they are not free. They are slaves to their possessions—stocks, bonds, cars, land—because their possessions consume them.

Of course, it's exciting to be blessed with the ability to make money. My father had that ability. He started out at age sixteen with a pickup truck and began to haul things for people in Argentina. When he made some money, he bought a piece of land. When he made more money, he bought more land. Eventually, he started a construction materials business, then began building and selling houses. Everything he did led to even greater money-making opportunities.

At the age of thirty-six, however, my father suddenly died. He left my mother with six children to support and a growing business to manage.

My mother knew nothing about business and my father hadn't left a will. In three short years, everything we had was gone. When my father was alive, our chauffeur would take my mother anywhere she wanted to go. Three years after my father died, she lived in a small house and was eight months behind in her rent.

I learned at an early age that material goods and all the status and pleasure that go with them can vanish quickly. We can be wealthy and respected by the community one day and be paupers the next.

While here on earth, Jesus commended those who used their possessions wisely, but He condemned those who selfishly hoarded their possessions. Therefore, we also are to be free with our possessions, not possessive of them. We are to give them away when we feel the Lord wants us to give them away. After all, they are not ours, but a gift from our Heavenly Father.

For a Christian, the real pleasure and joy of making money is in giving it away. But we often lose that pleasure by holding on to our possessions too tightly. And when we lose the possessions we've grasped so tightly, we suffer great depression.

When Pat and I went to Colombia to begin our first missionary term, we left many friends behind. Peter, one of those friends, had a small swimming pool cleaning business in California and helped support us.

After we had been in Colombia about three years, Peter's daughter came to visit us. We couldn't help but notice that she was very well dressed and seemed to have quite a bit of money. We didn't think much about it until we went back to the United States on furlough a year later. Peter met us at the airport, looking fantastic. He had a suntan, manicured nails, and perfectly styled hair. We left the airport in his new Lincoln Continental Mark IV.

Later, Peter took us out to his health club. We jogged, worked out, and relaxed in the Jacuzzi. Then we went to a fine restaurant for lunch, where we tried to catch up on the past four years.

"You know, Luis," Peter said, "I've come into a lot of money since you've been on the mission field. I don't clean pools anymore; I hire kids to do the work for me. I own some radio stations, an investment company, and hundreds of acres of oceanfront property. The Lord really has blessed me."

The blessing was evident. In four years, everything Peter touched had turned to profit.

"I really want to help you in your work, Luis," Peter continued. "I want to give you some money to help you get on television. As soon as I finish working out a few more business deals, I'll have plenty of money to invest in world evangelism. You'll be in great financial shape thanks to me. I should be able to make about half a million dollars on just one of those deals, and ten percent of it will be for you."

Well, that particular deal worked out. Peter made his $500,000. But as soon as that business venture was completed, another great opportunity came up.

"Luis," Peter said, "as soon as this next deal is finalized, I'll be able to give you even more money."

Great, I thought. *When this money comes through, I'll be able to devote even more time and energy to my work. Thanks to Peter, I won't have to spend as much time on fund-raising.*

Suddenly, however, economic recession hit the United States. Peter's financial empire crumbled. He lost millions of dollars and had nothing left to give to the Lord's work. When I saw him again, he was extremely depressed, regretting that he had not given his money to the Lord when he had it.

"What really eats me up," he said thoughtfully, "is that a bunch of bankers now have all the money I wanted to give to the Lord. And there's nothing I can do about it."

Here was a man who had millions of dollars and sincerely wanted to give it to the Lord's work. But he focused on ways to make more money, rather than how he could please the Lord with what he had. Too late, he learned that possessions can come to us one day and vanish the next.

In contrast, the loss of my father's wealth subtracted nothing from the eternal investment he made in the kingdom of God. I always knew my father was a generous man, but just within the past few years I have learned more about how much my father gave with eternity in view.

In Argentina recently, I met a man who was in the church where my father became a Christian. "Do you know that your father and Mr. Rogers (the man who led him to the Lord) started nine local churches in nine towns around your little town outside of Buenos Aires?" he said to me.

I said I thought it was seven.

"No, it was nine."

Then he said, "Did you know also that your dad built a chapel in each one of those towns?"

I didn't know that. I knew he built two.

"No, he built nine chapels."

My father was a Christian for only nine years. Each of those nine years, Mr. Rogers took my father to one of these towns. They had street meetings. They had tent meetings. And they would start a church—one a year.

And then my dad built a church building in each town—I didn't know that before.

The elderly man wasn't finished. Next he said, "Do you know that your dad used to give away houses all the time?"

I said I had heard about it.

"The house in which I still live your dad gave to me," he said. "I was a poor guy—he built a house and gave it to me. There are a lot of people who live in houses today that your dad built and just gave to them."

I couldn't believe it. I knew my dad made money, but giving away houses like that! I thought, *Wow! My dad was better than I even imagined.*

One of the greatest lessons we can learn is to keep eternity's values in full view. We are not to live for our possessions. We are not to devote our time and energy to amassing earthly treasures, to securing those things that moths and rust destroy (Matt. 6:20). Yes, my father's earthly fortune was lost, but how exciting that his eternal fortune continues to reap dividends!

When we live in the power of the indwelling Christ and are renewed every day, we will focus on the eternal reality of things we *cannot* see, rather than on the fleeting reality of the things we see on earth.

RENEWED CHRISTIANS HAVE NO FEAR OF THE FUTURE

As spiritually renewed Christians, we have a clear-minded confidence in the future because we know that heaven is real. Paul, who experienced many hardships during his life, describes the certainty of heaven:

> Now we know that if the earthly tent we live in is destroyed, we have a building from God, an eternal house in heaven, not built by human hands. Meanwhile we groan, longing to be clothed with our heavenly dwelling, because when we are clothed, we will not be found naked. For while we are in this tent, we groan and are burdened, because we do not wish to be unclothed but to be clothed with our heavenly

dwelling, so that what is mortal may be swallowed up by life. Now it
is God who has made us for this very purpose and has given us the Spirit
as a deposit, guaranteeing what is to come (2 Cor. 5:1–5).

This is one of the Bible's most beautiful passages. It's exciting to
know that God has an eternal home for Christians in the heavens! C. S.
Lewis once said, "No one is ready to live on earth until he's ready to live
in heaven." I believe he's absolutely right. Once we have established the
fact that our eternal home is in heaven, we can face life comfortably. We
know where we are going. We have peace because we know that when we
die we will be present with the Lord.

In this passage, Paul is saying several important things about our future
as Christians. First, he describes our earthly bodies as being tents. If
you've ever gone camping, you know what little protection a tent offers.
It flaps in the wind and can be flattened by a single gust. A tent can leak
in the rain and often is chilly. All in all, a tent is pretty fragile. Yet that's
how Paul describes our bodies. But he goes on to say that it's no big deal
if our tents are destroyed; God has built an eternal building in the heavens for us. What assurance!

When I was at Multnomah Biblical Seminary (then Multnomah
School of the Bible), Dr. Willard Aldrich served as its president. At the time,
his mother was almost ninety-six and Dr. Aldrich would visit her every day
at noon to feed and talk with her. Mrs. Aldrich dearly loved Jesus and was
waiting for Him to come again, as He promised.

One day, when Dr. Aldrich went to feed his mother, she did not want
to eat. She felt her time had come and asked Dr. Aldrich to pray that the
Lord would allow her to go to be with Him.

"Mother, I can't ask God to take you home," Dr. Aldrich explained.
"That's His business. Why don't I feed you a little soup, instead? After all,
you can't go to heaven on an empty stomach."

"No, Willard," she answered. "They will feed me as soon as I get there."

That evening, she went to be with the Lord.

What confidence! That's the way I'd like to go. I want to talk about
going to be with Jesus with the same assurance I have when I discuss any
activity I've planned. If we live in the power of the indwelling Christ, we
have an absolute assurance of the future. We know where we are going when
our life on earth is over.

Mrs. Aldrich isn't the only Christian to have known with certainty where she was going. Reading the biography of F. B. Meyer, I learned that one of the last postcards he wrote before he died read, "Dear Brother: I have raced you to heaven. I am just off. See you there. Love, F. B. Meyer." Obviously he and his friend had discussed the reality of heaven. They knew where they were going.

Paul also writes, "Our dying bodies make us groan and sigh" (2 Cor. 5:4 NLT). Isn't that the truth! Life isn't easy. We groan under the heavy load of problems and temptations that beset us, yet hope for the Second Coming of our Lord before we die. We long to go to the eternal place God has prepared for us.

Today, many Christians who are burdened with personal problems want only to hear sugar-coated solutions. Yet if they would look at life from God's perspective and truly believe in the reality of heaven, those same Christians would find the peace they seek.

I've heard that Andrew Bonar, a Scottish preacher and songwriter, would wake up every morning, open the front door, look up to the heavens, and say, "Lord Jesus, perhaps today." He understood and believed in the eternal hope Paul describes.

I have seen Christians live through intense suffering and anxiety in this present life while maintaining the certain hope of eternal life with God. Dr. Roy Kraft, former pastor of Twin Lakes Baptist Church in Santa Cruz, California, watched his oldest son, David, maintain this hope while suffering a slow and painful death.

Prior to his illness, David had been the perfect son. He had faithfully followed the Lord, pastored a small church, married a wonderful woman, and fathered two children. But then he contracted a rare and incurable form of cancer. When surgery confirmed this diagnosis, the hospital called Dr. Kraft to notify him that his son's cancer was, indeed, terminal. They also asked him to break the news to David.

When Dr. Kraft arrived at his son's hospital room, David asked everyone else to leave. After learning of his condition, David simply said, "Dad, come over here and put your arms around me. Hold me tight."

Then he said, "Dad, I want to tell you two things. First, I love you. And second, thank you for teaching me how to have a strong faith that is sufficient for times like this."

Shortly before David passed away, Dr. Kraft talked with his son about going home to glory. He mentioned that David soon would be seeing the Lord, and said, "When you see Jesus, tell Him I love Him too."

A few days later, after Dr. Kraft had taken David's children to see their father for the last time, he received a call in the night; his son had died. Yet Dr. Kraft told me he knew his son really was more alive in death than he ever could have been in life. How wonderful to know that no matter what we go through here on earth we have, without a doubt, a secure place with Jesus Christ in eternity.

In spite of the overwhelming certainty of heaven, God knew that we still would have a tendency to doubt this marvelous truth. So, as Paul explains, God sent the Holy Spirit to dwell within us as a guarantee of heaven (2 Cor. 5:5). He sent the Holy Spirit to be "Christ in you, the hope of glory" (Col. 1:27). God didn't have to do that for us. But He wanted to give us a continual assurance that heaven is our eternal home.

It is Jesus who makes the difference. Just before my own father died, he began to clap his hands and sing a song about heaven. Then his head fell on the pillow and he pointed up to heaven and said, "I'm going to be with Jesus, which is far better." Several hours later he was in heaven! Because my father had trusted Jesus Christ as Savior, he could face death with the absolute assurance he was going to heaven.

As Christians, it is our privilege to rejoice in the certainty of our eternal home in heaven. The world may laugh at us, but we can enjoy the blessing of that certain hope and live without fear of the future.

RENEWED CHRISTIANS AIM TO PLEASE GOD

When spiritual renewal is occurring in the life of a believer, he or she has no greater purpose than to please God. Look closely at what Paul writes in this passage:

> Therefore we are always confident and know that as long as we are at home in the body we are away from the Lord. We live by faith, not by sight. We are confident, I say, and would prefer to be away from the body and at home with the Lord. So we make it our goal to please him, whether we are at home in the body or away from it. For we must all appear before the judgment seat of Christ, that each one may receive what is due him for the things done while in the body, whether good or bad (2 Cor. 5:6–10).

Although we long for heaven, our purpose is to please God while we are here on earth. Whatever we do in life—whether it be running a business, studying, teaching, raising a family, preaching, relaxing, or serving others—we can have no higher purpose than to please Him.

When we aim to please God, Paul says we are "always confident." This means that we experience excitement and joy in all aspects of our lives. When we know we are pleasing Him, we are successful by God's standards. Therefore, we can walk confidently by faith, no matter what opposition we encounter or what criticism is directed at us. Even the ups and downs of life can be exciting; we know a sovereign God is molding our character so we can bring greater glory to Him.

It's difficult to be depressed or embittered if we are being renewed on a daily basis through the power of the indwelling Christ. When our purpose is to please the Lord, we can't be held down. We're a bit like corks floating in water. They can be pushed down, but always will pop right back up to the surface.

When we please God, we have peace. We're not trying to juggle a dozen different things in order to please everyone around us. Instead, we have a single purpose—to please God.

When we try to please ourselves or others, however, things get out of balance. Far too many of us have become overly involved in various causes and have lost our perspective. Our priorities no longer are established by God, but by many clamoring voices, which may be sincere and good. We have forgotten that our purpose is to please God.

But as spiritually renewed Christians who aim to please God, we can walk with security and confidence. We no longer view life and its problems with the shortsighted limitations of a merely human perspective. Instead, we view life with the long-term assurance that comes only from God's eternal perspective.

FOR PERSONAL REFLECTION

Read 2 Corinthians 4:17–5:10.

1. "We too easily forget that our primary purpose on earth—our all-consuming passion—should be to please God." How would you describe your primary passion in life?

2. "God's eternal perspective enables us to see beyond the hazards of our future here on earth to the certainty of everlasting life with Him." How does God's perspective enable you to endure troubles? To handle possessions? If it doesn't, what needs to change?

3. "I want to talk about going to be with Jesus with the same assurance I have when I discuss any activity I've planned." How do you talk about your future in heaven?

4. "When we please God, we have peace. We're not trying to juggle a dozen different things in order to please everyone around us." Make a list of all the people you are trying to please (including yourself). How do these efforts compare to pleasing God? How can pleasing God bring you peace?

FOR INTERACTIVE DISCUSSION

Read aloud 2 Corinthians 4:17–5:10.

1. "When our primary aim as Christians is to please God, we can focus our lives on the concerns of God, instead of allowing the world's concerns to distract us." How does the world distract *you personally* from your purpose of pleasing God? How do both problems and possessions prove to be temporary rather than eternal?

2. "When we live in the power of the indwelling Christ and are renewed every day, we will focus on the eternal reality of things we *cannot* see, rather than on the fleeting reality of what we see on earth." What are the realities and values of eternity? How do we invest our lives and our belongings in light of these values?

3. "As spiritually renewed Christians, we have a clear-minded confidence in the future because we know that heaven is real." How does a complete confidence in the reality of heaven contribute to spiritual renewal?

4. "When we know we are pleasing to Him, we are successful by God's standards." By whose standards do you feel successful? How can we know we are pleasing God?

CHAPTER 10

Living to Please God

oday, in an effort to be sophisticated and contemporary, many Christians have stopped trying to persuade others to follow Jesus Christ. There's an underlying feeling in our society that nice people just don't go around persuading other people to do things. Some folks seem to think that convincing others to follow Christ is the same as ramming the Gospel down their throats. As a result, they shy away from witnessing, thinking that living a comfortable Christian life is good enough.

Other Christians, who believe that salvation is totally a result of God's intervention, feel no need to persuade others to follow Christ.

However, communicating the message of Jesus Christ—persuading others to repent and believe—is the primary objective of every spiritually renewed Christian. And it is something that always pleases our Heavenly Father.

Paul explains the importance of persuading others:

> Since, then, we know what it is to fear the Lord, we try to persuade men. What we are is plain to God, and I hope it is also plain to your conscience. We are not trying to commend ourselves to you again, but are giving you an opportunity to take pride in us, so that you can answer those who take pride in what is seen rather than in what

is in the heart. If we are out of our mind, it is for the sake of God; if we are in our right mind, it is for you (2 Cor. 5:11–13).

Paul is saying, in essence, that some people will consider anyone who witnesses a lunatic. But that's OK with Paul. To those who would accuse him of madness, he says, "That's OK. If I'm crazy, it's for God." Paul decided that if people were going to think him crazy, and his perceived craziness was the result of his being obedient to God, that was acceptable to him.

Every Christian today must make the same decision. We must decide whether we are willing to obey God and persuade others to follow Christ—despite the cost. Once we've decided to ignore insults and misperceptions, we are free to persuade others. But until we make that decision, we will be cowards—hesitant to witness to anyone.

Of course, we really don't persuade others through our own efforts; we allow the indwelling Christ to persuade others through us. We are happy and willing subjects, allowing the Lord to use our intellectual abilities, emotions, and verbal faculties as instruments of persuasion.

Billy Graham is a great example of a person who pleases God by persuading others. Dr. Graham is in his eighties, has more than a dozen grandchildren, and has been preaching for more than fifty years. Because of his Parkinson's disease, he preaches at only one or two major meetings a year. But when he stands to pray for a nation or give the Gospel message one more time, his voice carries the same passion and longing for each person listening to come to Jesus Christ.

You don't have to be a world-famous evangelist to persuade others for Jesus Christ. Each time my team and I go to a city for one of our evangelistic festivals, we ask people to pray for five friends or family members they would like to see come to Christ. We have found that many people don't wait for the festival and my message to lead their loved ones to Jesus Christ. As they pray, God gives them the opportunity and the spiritual ability to persuade others. Persuading others to follow Christ is our greatest work

When it comes to evangelism, many of us don't like to believe what the Bible says. We rather would believe philosophers and intellectuals who discourage us from "imposing" the Gospel on others. We're tempted to believe the lie promoted by Bertrand Russell and others that living the "good life" is good enough.

But we all have sinned and come short of the glory of God (Rom. 3:23). All of us have gone astray. Without Christ, no one can have eternal life. No matter how beautiful or self-assured a person may be on the outside, a vacuum may still exist on the inside—a void that only Jesus Christ can fill. That's why persuading others to follow God is so important. Several barriers, however, can prevent Christians from fulfilling this responsibility.

Today, even in Christian circles, some people think we don't need to witness because the lost are happy "just as they are." People who believe that are pretty naive.

When Pat and I lived in Mexico City—a modern, cosmopolitan city—we saw people who had every good thing this world could offer, yet suffered deeply inside. At the hairdresser's, for example, Pat noticed many of the middle-class women spoke with a slur. Later, she discovered these women were addicted to tranquilizers. They obviously were not satisfied with life and hoped to fill their emptiness through artificial means.

Some individuals believe that if we really care about people, we should do everything we can for them except preach the Gospel. A university professor once asked me, "Palau, how can you go to Latin America, where they have so many economic and social problems, and preach about the resurrected Christ? Isn't there anything more practical you can do for those people?"

"No," I said. "There is no better way to help them. You can help hungry people in a material way, and we do. But the people of this world have created the problems of this world. If we can lead them to Christ, we can create a climate for other positive, practical changes to take place."

In some Latin American countries, a man's masculinity is measured by the number of children he fathers. He is considered especially *macho* if he has those children by many different women. As a result, many children in these countries are illegitimate, and this creates tremendous social and economic pressures. These men also squander much of their income on alcohol, gambling, and prostitutes, further diminishing their ability to care for their families.

When such men are persuaded to place their trust in Jesus Christ, a dramatic change takes place. For one, they become concerned about the welfare of their families. By giving up alcohol, womanizing, and gambling, they can save as much as fifty percent of their income and use it to meet their families' needs. This change not only brings immediate benefits to the family, but serves as an example to the community of what the power of God can do in a person's life.

Another barrier to persuading others to follow Christ is "sophistication." That is, as we adopt our culture's values, we find it increasingly difficult to persuade others. We don't want to offend people, appear strange, or lose a newfound status. So we do nothing.

I, too, have been guilty of this. My next-door neighbor in Mexico City was a young television personality. We would chat from time to time, and he mentioned that he listened to our radio program occasionally. But I didn't share the Gospel of Christ with him. *After all,* I thought, *he seems completely immune to the problems of life.* He was a playboy-type who lived the "good life." He apparently didn't care a great deal about spiritual values.

My neighbor eventually married a bright college graduate. After his wedding, everything still seemed to be going great for him. He and his wife would leave for work together, laughing and talking.

Suddenly, though, my neighbor changed. The joy seemed to have left his face. He and his wife started driving separate cars to work. I could tell their marriage was souring, and I felt the need to talk to him, but I didn't want to meddle in his life. I went about my business and headed off for a crusade in Peru. After all, that was the polite thing to do. When I returned home, I learned that my neighbor had killed himself. I was heartbroken. I knew I should have gone to him and persuaded him to repent and follow Christ. But because of false courtesy—because I followed a social norm—I didn't do it.

It's very convenient to make excuses for not persuading others to follow Christ. We may say we don't want to be overbearing or offensive. We may think we can't possibly witness to a person because he or she will become angry. But when we approach life's situations with the absolute conviction that we are to persuade others about Christ, we will have courage. We will discover that people are open to the Gospel message.

Over the years I have learned that some of the people I thought would be most closed to the Gospel often are the most receptive. Although they may outwardly fear it, in their hearts they welcome the message of the Gospel.

When my wife and I were in the United Kingdom, the lord mayor of a large city invited us to dinner. When we met him, his hands were literally trembling. He obviously was very nervous. We sat down, and he offered me a drink.

"No, thank you," I said, so he poured himself one. In fact, I learned later that he had been so nervous about our meeting he had had six drinks before I arrived!

We talked for a bit, then went into the dining room for dinner. As we joked and told stories, the lord mayor began to relax. The reason for his nervousness soon became evident.

"I had a different idea of what an evangelist would be like," he said, finishing his dessert. "I thought you'd try to convert me right on the spot."

"No," I replied, "I take my time." We had developed a good enough rapport by this time that I felt free to joke with him.

As we talked, he pointed to the cross he wore around his neck, his symbol of authority. "You know," he said thoughtfully, "I'm going to take this cross off. I wore it because I thought it would impress you. But I don't have to impress you, do I?"

"No, you don't," I replied.

"We've had dinner together," he then said, "and you still haven't told me what you believe. Will you tell me now?"

At his invitation, I shared the Gospel with him. He didn't open his heart to Jesus Christ that night. But I knew that by being sensitive to his defensiveness, I still was able to share God's message with him and please my Heavenly Father.

More recently, I was flying from New Delhi to Calcutta to meet with Christian leaders regarding a possible evangelistic festival there. The fellow beside me looked like an educated man. I wasn't planning to start the conversation, but he began chatting and I found out that he was a lawyer. He asked me who I was and where I was going.

I have a style of breaking the news slowly so as not to shock people. If I say, "I'm an evangelist," they fall apart. And so I usually say, "My job is to help people with their troubles—in their marriages and families and personal lives," which is true. So finally they say, "Well, how do you help them?"

That is when I reply that I help them from the Bible and the Good News message of Jesus Christ.

When I told the lawyer this, he immediately said, "I thought so. I looked at you, and you've got an aura above you."

I thought, *What a deal. Take a picture. My mother would be delighted.*

Then instantly he said, "I'd give anything to travel with someone like you and help people." He told me all about his guru in southern India and our conversation continued on a spiritual track.

That's what I love about the people of India—they're so spiritually sensitive. They think about their gods all the time. Their idolatry may seem like a huge obstacle to the Gospel, but even educated people are willing to get into a discussion about spiritual issues just like that. Then you have the opportunity to introduce them to the God of the universe and His Son, Jesus Christ.

Perhaps the people in your life are not so willing to discuss spiritual truths. But as renewed Christians, our responsibility is simply to be obedient and available for God's use. When our aim is to please God, we have a firm determination to persuade others to follow Jesus Christ. That conviction gives direction and joy to life. No matter where we work or what we do, we have an objective that stands above all else to persuade others to follow Christ.

WHY WE PERSUADE OTHERS

Although we've touched on it briefly, let's now look at one question in more detail. What motivates a Christian to persuade others to follow Christ? One answer is found in Paul's observation, "For Christ's love compels us" (2 Cor. 5:14).

As Christians, our primary motivation to persuade others comes from Christ's love within us. When we see people suffering, we want to reach out and help. When we see teenagers without any biblical orientation adopting secular philosophies, we want to bring them into the safety of the kingdom of God. When we see married couples' lives falling apart, we want to counsel them and show them the biblical hope of a life together in Christ.

We don't persuade others because we want to win an argument, because we think we are better than anyone else, or because we want to clobber others over the head with biblical truth. We persuade others because the love of Christ flows through us, giving us compassion for the lost. We reach out and share the love of Christ with others because His love has done so much for us.

Jesus Christ has given me a marvelous life. It hasn't always been easy, but I have seen the truth of Matthew 6:33—"But seek first his kingdom and his righteousness, and all these things will be given to you as well," and of Psalm 37:4—"Delight yourself in the LORD and he will give you the desires of your heart." I have seen the promises of these verses fulfilled in my own life, and the lives of thousands of others who have surrendered to Christ. We are free from immorality, hatred, guilt, and other destructive practices that ensnare people.

While in Ecuador, I had the privilege of sharing the love of Christ with an air force colonel, one of three men governing the country at that time. At first I didn't know who he was. He came into our counseling center to talk to me.

"You have forty-five minutes," he said. "If you can give me the answer to my problems, I'll accept Christ. If not, I'm going to kill myself."

Somewhat stunned, I asked him to tell me about his problems.

"I am forty-two years old and a very important man in this country," he said. "But I've had an emptiness within me since I was a boy, and I can no longer live with it.

"I married young, but my wife and I had problems, so I divorced her. I married again, but I still have the same problems. So the problem must not be with my wives. It must be with me.

"When I watched you on television last night, you said that Christ is alive and that He can change a man's life. Now tell me the honest truth. Do you really believe that Christ is alive? Can He really change a man's life?"

"Yes, I believe that," I said, and proceeded to share many promises of Scripture with him. We then prayed, and the colonel invited Christ into his life.

Before he left, I asked him why he had come to talk with me. He told me that when he was a young boy, he and his parents were traveling from their home in the mountains to Quito, the capital city. But his alcoholic father became so sick on the train he could no longer travel. They had to get off the train in a strange village. The only people in the village who helped them were two young European women, who took the family to their home, prayed for the father, and gave him medicine. After three months of care, the father was well enough to travel.

Although the colonel was only three years old at that time, he never forgot the love of those two women. Forty years later, the Christlike love of those women paid off. The colonel became a Christian.

When the love of Christ controls us, we have an unselfish compulsion that moves us to persuade others. However, this compulsion to love and persuade others doesn't come overnight. It's hard, for instance, to love people who are arrogant, who misuse or abuse other people, or flagrantly violate God's laws. But when we spend time before God in prayer, He will give us the ability to look beyond the mask those people wear and give us a burden for the hurting person inside.

Ray Stedman, the pastor who first brought me to the United States and was like a father to me, was an expert at seeing behind people's masks. Observing some of his counseling sessions, I was amazed at his ability to discover the core of each person's problem. One day I asked him how he did it.

"Luis," he explained, "once you get behind someone's mask there's basically one problem—ego. No matter how many long stories people have developed to excuse their problems, you will always find their difficulties are ego-centered. But if you can help ego-centered people become Christ-centered people, all their long stories will fade away."

That lesson has helped me tremendously. Whenever I sit with an oppressive Latin American politician (or a morally questionable American politician), I have a choice. I can blast that person for all the wrong things he is doing and alienate him from the Gospel of Christ, or I can allow myself to love the lost person behind the terrible mask and possibly win him to Jesus Christ.

We must not allow ourselves to become hardened to Christ's love for the lost. Whenever I begin to lose my compassion for the lost, I remember an experience of one of our former team members in Bogota, Colombia.

Thousands of children are abandoned on the streets of Bogota. Many of them are sexually abused. They sleep in doorways and abandoned buildings and steal food to stay alive. It's heartbreaking to see these precious children and be unable to help all of them.

One day, while walking through Bogota, Don Fults saw a group of excited street children dragging a cardboard box behind them. He asked them what was happening.

"We have a baby in the box!" they exclaimed.

Don couldn't quite believe it, so he pulled some dirty rags aside and found a newborn baby. The children had taken a soda pop bottle, filled it with who-knows-what, stuffed a rag in the top, and given it to the baby. The infant was trying to suck on the bottle.

"Where did you find the baby?" Don asked.

"In the garbage," the children replied. "It was still alive, so we're going to take care of it."

Whenever I remember this story, I think and pray, *God, give me compassion. Those little street children had more love for an abandoned baby than their parents had for them. How can I harden my heart against the lost? May the love of Christ control me and flow through me.*

Why do we persuade people? As we've already discussed, we persuade others because we know the love of Christ and know what our God will do for them. But there's a second reason for persuading others: "Since, then, we know what it is to fear the Lord, we try to persuade men" (2 Cor. 5:11).

In this verse, Paul is saying that we persuade others because we fear God. We tend to think of fear as a negative motivation. But the Apostle Paul really is saying, "Look, we will face Christ in eternity. At judgment, He will hold us accountable for persuading others. I don't want to face Christ in eternity and have to explain why I didn't obey Him and preach the Gospel to everyone. Therefore, you'd better believe I'm going to persuade others!"

The Lord isn't going to excuse us for disobeying His command to witness to others. Before the Judgment Seat of Christ we will have to answer for everything we have done, whether it be for good or evil.

Yes, the love of Christ moves us to persuade others. We don't want others to go to hell. We want them to enjoy full life in Christ and look forward to eternity with God. But we also persuade others, even when we don't want to, because we are under the authority of Christ, who says, "Do it!" Either we are available to God and are obedient to Him, or we are rebellious, refusing to persuade others.

HOW WE PERSUADE OTHERS

Most of us are quite aware of the limitations of our love. And it takes an incredible amount of love and commitment to persuade others to follow Christ. How, then, can we obtain the deep love and commitment required to persuade others? Paul points us to the answer:

For Christ's love compels us, because we are convinced that one

died for all, and therefore all died. And he died for all, that those who
live should no longer live for themselves but for him who died for them
and was raised again (2 Cor. 5:14–15).

To persuade others, the key is that we no longer live for ourselves; we
live for God. When we live for Him, we have an absolute unity of purpose.
The love of Christ flows through us, giving us compassion for the lost and
moving us to share Jesus Christ with others.

When we live for Him, all our knowledge, all our money, and all our
physical abilities belong to God. Life becomes exciting. We have tremendous purpose in persuading others to come to Christ, and through the Holy
Spirit, we receive the love that compels us to persuade them.

I firmly believe many Christians today do not enjoy the fullness of
Christ because they're living for themselves. What a waste! When we live
for ourselves, we become depressed. We lose the joy of the Lord. We don't
much care what happens to anyone else. We care only about ourselves.

When we live for Christ, although we may have successful business-
es or careers, our personal success isn't an end in itself. Our success is to
live a life that pleases God.

Years ago, while speaking at a series of church meetings in New York,
I talked with a sixty-seven-year-old doctor. One of the most distinguished
and respected ophthalmologists in the world, he had written classic texts
on eye care. When we were alone, he said, "Young man, I have a question
to ask. I will make a big decision on the basis of the answer you give me.

"When I was a young man at the university, I felt God calling me to
Afghanistan to help people with their eye problems. I even made a commitment to serve Christ by helping those who were sick.

"But after I graduated I married a woman from a fine family who
didn't share my commitment. When I mentioned going to the mission
field, she joined my in-laws and other acquaintances in telling me it was
a silly thing to do. They believed becoming a medical missionary would
be a waste of my educational investment. So I didn't go. That was forty-
two years ago, and I haven't had one day of peace since.

"But now I am retired and free to do what I believe God has called
me to do. I want to go to Afghanistan, but my wife still is against it. She
will not go. In fact, she slipped on the ice the other day and is acting as
if she has a broken leg. I have taken X-rays and know the leg is not bro-

ken. She is just using this mishap as an excuse not to go. Tell me, young man, at this late hour in my life, shall I stay or shall I go? Whatever you tell me I will do."

Whew! I thought. *Who am I to make such a decision for this man?* But as I considered and prayed about his situation, I put my arm around him and said, "Brother, you go."

Immediately he put his arms around me and began to cry. "Thank you, thank you," he wept. "I'm going. No one will stop me. If my wife doesn't want to go, she can stay here. But I am going to Afghanistan!"

The next day, the doctor still was excited, like a teenager in love. A few weeks later he—and his wife—went to Afghanistan. They made several trips ministering to the physical and spiritual needs of the people, and even his wife became excited about the work the Lord had given them.

The next time I saw him, his physical condition had greatly deteriorated. But he was very happy. He even asked me to give him "one of those big Latin hugs." Before we parted, though, he said, "The next time I see you, it will be in the presence of the King!" A short time after our meeting, he died.

I will always remember three things about his story. First, it must have been horrible for him to live for forty-two years without any peace because he had rebelled against God. Second, it's never too late to begin to follow God's will. Third, how wonderful it is to live for God, even after many years of disobedience, to be able to say, "Next time I see you, it will be in the presence of the King."

Every Christian must choose, more than once, whether to live for self or for God. That choice makes all the difference. When I think of the lifelong significance of choosing to please God, I think of George Beverly Shea.

Mr. Shea made the choice to live for God when he was a young man in New York City. He and a friend sold insurance during the week and sang at evangelistic street meetings on Sundays. A well-known producer heard them sing one evening and offered them a contract to perform on a television program. He also offered them a substantial amount of money, far more than they would earn selling insurance. They said they would pray about it.

Mr. Shea and his friend were very excited about the idea, but as they prayed, they didn't have peace about taking the job. Nothing was wrong with the program; it just didn't seem right. So Mr. Shea decided to continue singing at evangelistic meetings. His friend, however, took the television job and soon became well known in the industry.

Mr. Shea eventually began singing for WMBI, the Moody Bible Institute radio station in Chicago. And after Billy Graham heard him singing on that station, he invited Mr. Shea to join his evangelistic team. As a result of his commitment, George Beverly Shea has ministered to millions of people around the world and has sold millions of records. What an influence he has had on the world because he chose to live for Christ!

And what happened to his friend? He dropped out of sight. Years later, Mr. Shea learned that his old friend—with whom he once proclaimed the Gospel on the streets of New York City—was performing in a nightclub.

We all must choose whether we will live for Christ or for ourselves. It's horrifying to realize the lifelong consequences of seemingly simple decisions. We must be careful not to live for ourselves, but for Him who died and rose again.

When we live to please Him, the life of Christ keeps flowing through us—giving us compassion for the lost and the fear of the Lord that compels us to persuade others to follow Him.

FOR PERSONAL REFLECTION

Read 2 Corinthians 5:11–15.

1. "Once we've decided to ignore insults and misperceptions, we are free to persuade others." How do people react when you share the Gospel? How does this influence your response—and your efforts?

2. "When our aim is to please God, we have a firm determination to persuade others to follow Jesus Christ." How does your desire to please God motivate you to spread the Good News?

3. "When the love of Christ controls us, we have an unselfish compulsion that moves us to persuade others." How does Christ's love motivate and compel you?

4. "To persuade others, the key is that we no longer live for ourselves; we live for God; . . . many Christians today do not enjoy the fullness of Christ because they're living for *themselves*." How do you feel and act when you are living to please yourself? To please others? To please God?

FOR INTERACTIVE DISCUSSION

Read aloud 2 Corinthians 5:11–15.

1. "There's an underlying feeling in our society that nice people just don't go around persuading other people to do things." Why does our society frown on persuading others to change? In light of this, how can we best persuade others to trust Jesus Christ for salvation?

2. "Some individuals believe that if we really care about people, we should do everything we can for them except preach the Gospel." How is sharing the Gospel with people the most loving way we can help them?

3. "Over the years I have learned that some of the people I thought would be most closed to the Gospel often are the most receptive." What groups or individuals that you know seem the most closed to the Gospel? In what ways may they actually welcome it? How can we change our approach to these resistant people?

4. "It takes an incredible amount of love and commitment to persuade others to follow Christ. How, then, can we obtain the deep love and commitment required to persuade others?"

CHAPTER 11

Serving as Ambassadors

As human beings, we naturally have an ego-centered perspective of other human beings. That is, we perceive others in terms of their relationship to us. We may, for example, see others as sources of revenue, sources of pleasure, sources of irritation, or whatever seems appropriate at the moment.

When we live for Christ rather than for ourselves, however, we gain a new, divine perspective of people. An almost imperceptible change occurs in our hearts; we want to persuade others to follow Christ. We realize that behind the makeup, behind the brusque manner, behind the efficient homemaker, behind the rising executive, there are real people who need Jesus Christ.

Paul describes how our perspectives change when we begin to live for Christ:

> So from now on we regard no one from a worldly point of view. Though we once regarded Christ in this way, we do so no longer. Therefore, if anyone is in Christ, he is a new creation; the old has gone, the new has come! (2 Cor. 5:16–17).

Our view of Christ changes when we begin to live for Him. We focus less on His human dimension and more on His divine, eternal dimension. We realize that Christ has made a tremendous difference in our lives; we see Him not only as our Savior, but also as our very source of eternal life.

When we live for Christ and adopt God's eternal perspective, we begin to see people in a different light as well. For instance, if a coworker's mannerisms or actions have bothered us, our annoyance at that person fades away when we realize his or her need for God. We begin to think, *What would that person be like if Christ took over his or her life?*

Through God's perspective, we begin to love that person, not because we have such a great ability to love, but because the indwelling Christ moves us to love. We begin to care deeply for that person, wanting to see him or her come to Christ. We have a vision for the new creature Christ will create no matter how egocentric, materialistic, or hateful that person currently may be.

When we live for Christ, we also view new Christians from God's perspective. Instead of concentrating on their relative spiritual immaturity, we remember what they would be like if Christ had *not* entered their lives. Thus we can rejoice in the new creatures God has made.

THE MIRACLE OF RECONCILIATION

At times, we may be tempted to think that some people have been so horrible, have done so much harm to others, or have been so stubborn in their rejection of God that even if they become Christians, they never will change. Such is not the case. When Christ's blood makes us new creatures, we have a new relationship with God (2 Cor. 5:17); we are reconciled to Him regardless of our past sins. Paul explains what this reconciliation means:

> All this is from God, who reconciled us to himself through Christ and gave us the ministry of reconciliation: that God was reconciling the world to himself in Christ, not counting men's sins against them. And he has committed to us the message of reconciliation (2 Cor. 5:18–19).

On the cross, Jesus Christ took away all the guilt, passion, bitterness, jealousy, pride, and emptiness that separate us from God. When His blood was poured out, we were cleansed from our sin—all of it, even the horrible, shameful sins we can't admit to anyone else.

I don't fully understand how the blood of Christ cleanses us, but I do believe the Bible when it says His blood cleanses us and reconciles us to God. As the old-time preachers used to say, "I don't understand how a black cow eats green grass and produces white milk and yellow butter. But I drink the milk and I eat the butter just the same."

You and I may not be able to keep up with the rapid advances of technology. Before we have time to understand the workings of a fax machine, electronic mail, cellular telephones, and instant messaging become commonplace. Now, I don't understand how all these electronic gadgets work, but I'm more than happy to put them to use to make my life easier. Whether or not we fully understand the mystery of our forgiveness, we can make it real in our lives.

Through the miraculous cleansing of Christ's blood, we become new creatures; we are reconciled to God. Many times I have witnessed the dramatic changes that take place in a person when he or she is reconciled to God. Let me share one of those experiences with you.

After hearing me lead a young woman to Christ during an HCJB radio program in Ecuador, a woman with a high-pitched, squeaky voice telephoned me, requesting an appointment. As soon as we scheduled it, she thanked me and abruptly hung up.

The next morning, as I waited for her, I saw a little woman accompanied by two burly men walk through the gates of HCJB. The men remained outside as the woman entered my office.

"Do the gentlemen want to come in?" I asked.

"Nope," the woman replied, with the same squeaky voice I remembered from the night before. Without another word, she proceeded to search my office. She checked under the desk and looked behind the pictures, apparently searching for electronic "bugs." Meanwhile, one of her companions moved to a position near the gate. The other one stood just outside my office door.

This lady is crazy, I thought.

She sat down, crossed her legs like a man, began smoking, and started verbally attacking me. For twenty-five minutes she cursed and swore, telling me what a bunch of deceptive liars, thieves, and crooks all preachers and priests were.

As I listened and watched her light one cigarette after another I prayed,

Lord, how shall I handle this? Finally I said, "Madam, can I help you?"

Suddenly she started to cry. She sobbed for five minutes. Then she said, "In the thirty-eight years of my life, you are the first person who has ever wanted to help me. Everyone else has said, 'Help me with this. Help me with that. Please come here and do this.'" Then she cried some more.

"What is your name?" I asked.

"Why do you want to know my name?" she snapped.

"Well, we're talking," I replied, "and I'd like to know who I'm talking with."

"My name is Maria Benitez-Perez," she replied. "I'm secretary of the Communist Party here in Ecuador. I'm a Marxist-Leninist. I don't believe in God." And she started insulting me again.

When she cooled down a bit I asked, "Did you come here to insult me, or do you want me to help you?"

She began to tell me her life story. It took three and one-half hours to tell it all! I listened carefully so I would know how to help her.

The daughter of a wealthy and prominent family, Maria had rebelled as a teenager. Since her family was very religious, she had attended a Catholic boarding school, but refused to stay there. Her parents gave her an ultimatum: go to school or leave the house. She left.

Eventually, the communists befriended her and she joined their organization. Soon thereafter she married a medical student, had a baby, then divorced her husband. She married again, had another child, divorced, and married a third time. After that, she lived a sexually promiscuous life.

But that wasn't all. Maria had stabbed a man—one of her communist comrades—who later committed suicide. Some of her friends were killed in riots she incited; Maria survived only because she hid when the situation became dangerous.

Maria told me how she laughed at and mocked the Catholic bishop as he performed her mother's funeral service. As she related her actions at her mother's funeral, she softened.

"Even though I don't believe in God," she said, "I've always felt guilty about the way I behaved at the funeral." She paused for a moment. "But supposing there were a God, do you think He'd forgive me and receive me like you told that woman last night?"

Aha! I thought. *Now I know how to help this woman.* I've learned that one of the best ways to minister to a professing atheist is to take one verse from the Bible and repeat its message over and over again until it sticks. So I selected the beautiful promise of Hebrews 10:17 to share with her.

"Yes," I said. "But don't just take my word for it. Listen to what God says: 'Their sins and lawless acts I will remember no more.'"

"But listen," she protested. "I've told you all about my life. Look at what I've done!"

I repeated Hebrews 10:17. She protested again and again. Each time I repeated the same verse—seventeen times in all—before she was ready to ask Christ to forgive her.

Finally she said, "If God could forgive me, it would be the greatest miracle in the world."

We prayed together and she accepted Christ. A week later, before I left Ecuador, I saw her again. She was a changed person. She looked happy and had a peaceful spirit.

When Jesus Christ took that wild Ecuadorian Marxist and made her into a new woman, He accomplished the same work in her life that He accomplishes in the life of every Christian. He reconciled her to God.

Until we come to Christ, we are rebels. We may be very nice, gentle, educated rebels, but we are rebels nonetheless. When we surrender to Jesus Christ, however, we are reconciled to God. Through Jesus' death on the cross, our debt of sin is wiped out. No matter how many times we have dishonored God, He forgives us and sets us free from our passions, sets us free from all the masks we have worn to impress others.

Paul also says that God has entrusted His message of reconciliation to us (2 Cor. 5:19). I believe God's message of reconciliation refers not only to the lost, but also to believers.

Many forces of separation and division are at work in the body of Christ. It is a blessing to be peacemakers and see the body brought together in love despite the political, doctrinal, social, and economic barriers that threaten to divide it.

When the war between Argentina and Britain broke out in 1982, I was in Panama, involved in a congress with three hundred Christian leaders from the Spanish-speaking world. When we learned about the war, no one knew what to say or do. But two young British men who came to the congress presented a scroll to the meeting's Argentinean delegation, signed by several thousand British young people. The scroll read, "We love you in Jesus Christ. We are one in Jesus Christ. We are praying for you!"

The young men also brought an offering for the Argentinean Christians. That is what the ministry of reconciliation is all about!

ONCE RECONCILED, WE ARE AMBASSADORS

Once we are reconciled to God, we become His ambassadors. We represent Christ to the world so that the world might accept God's grace and be reconciled to Him. Paul succinctly describes the purpose of our ambassadorship:

> We are therefore Christ's ambassadors, as though God were making his appeal through us. We implore you on Christ's behalf: Be reconciled to God. God made him who had no sin to be sin for us, so that in him we might become the righteousness of God. As God's fellow workers, we urge you not to receive God's grace in vain. For he says, "In the time of my favor I heard you, and in the day of salvation I helped you." I tell you, now is the time of God's favor, now is the day of salvation (2 Cor. 5:20–6:2).

Have you ever seen an ambassador in action? When I was at Cardiff Castle in Wales, I saw the Japanese ambassador arrive for a meeting with British officials. What an impressive sight! A band played near the entrance to the castle. Banners and flags waved in the breeze. As we watched, a long, black limousine with flags mounted on its front fenders pulled up to the entrance. We were pushed aside as the ambassador stepped out of the limousine. All the officials of the city, who were dressed in their proper historical costumes, greeted the ambassador and ushered him into the castle.

An ambassador is treated with respect because, although he is a foreigner in a strange land, he represents his government. In this passage Paul says that every believer is an ambassador for Christ. In light of our eternal home, we are foreigners in the world; yet God has given us the responsibility and authority to be ambassadors of His kingdom. No matter what our background, status, or natural sphere of influence, we are ambassadors of God. He has given us power and authority to "make His appeal through us"—to persuade others to come to Christ.

As ambassadors of Jesus Christ we don't do whatever we please. We aren't ambassadors to serve our own egos. We are ambassadors for God— who speaks through us. We are to speak with authority and reveal His glory.

People aren't going to listen to us very long or pay much attention to what we say if we're just ordinary human beings. But when we speak in the power of the Holy Spirit, truth and authority fill our words. Unbelievers may try to deny the validity of our message, but in their hearts they know we speak the truth. They cannot escape Christ's message.

My friend Bud McWethy took his ambassadorship seriously. The last time I talked to Bud, during the last week of his life on earth, I knew he had been praying for me that morning.

"You're leaving for Hong Kong," he said.

I thought, *Bud is dying of cancer, and he knows my schedule?* I was amazed—but not really surprised. Right until the end, world evangelism remained his priority.

I met this North Dakota businessman not long after he trusted Jesus Christ as his Savior. During a trip to Latin America, Bud heard our program on HCJB and wrote to me. Over the years, he and his wife, Mary, traveled to several crusades to encourage me and watch as God changed lives through the Gospel. He served many years on our ministry's board of directors.

About two years before he died, Bud knew the end was approaching ever faster, yet he was in absolute peace. He said he wasn't "fighting cancer." He believed the Lord had a purpose in his illness. In his final moments he said to the hospice worker who was caring for him, "My work is finished."

What was Bud's work? Bud wanted people to know he was going to heaven—and he wanted them to come too. "When you speak at my burial," he told me, "tell people how to be sure they have eternal life and give them a chance to open their hearts to Jesus Christ." He arranged to have a special edition of my evangelistic booklet *What Is a Real Christian?* distributed at his funeral. As an ambassador for Jesus Christ, Bud put his Lord first throughout his physical life and beyond.

Every Christian is an ambassador for Jesus Christ. God can speak directly to people, but He usually speaks through His ambassadors. No matter how recently we may have come to know Christ, no matter how great or small our desire to be ambassadors, we are ambassadors. We have a tremendous privilege to represent the King of kings as we go through life. Regardless of our social status or occupation, the Bible says we have a position of authority and influence. Like Bud McWethy, we must take that position seriously.

As Ambassadors We Will Face Trouble

In spite of the dignity, honor, and respect shown ambassadors, most of them face incredible struggles. It isn't all parties, speeches, and receptions. In this day of international terrorism, some ambassadors are attacked, kidnapped, and held hostage.

Ambassadors for Christ's kingdom face difficult struggles too. In spite of the dignity we have as ambassadors of Christ, Paul warns us that we will face obstacles and trouble.

> We put no stumbling block in anyone's path, so that our ministry will not be discredited. Rather, as servants of God we commend ourselves in every way: in great endurance; in troubles, hardships and distresses; in beatings, imprisonments and riots; in hard work, sleepless nights and hunger; in purity, understanding, patience and kindness; in the Holy Spirit and in sincere love; in truthful speech and in the power of God; with weapons of righteousness in the right hand and in the left; through glory and dishonor, bad report and good report; genuine, yet regarded as impostors; known, yet regarded as unknown; dying, and yet we live on; beaten, and yet not killed; sorrowful, yet always rejoicing; poor, yet making many rich; having nothing, and yet possessing everything (2 Cor. 6:3–10).

That's the description of Paul fulfilling his ambassadorial duties!

Yes, being an ambassador of Christ will cost something, but there also is much to gain. As ambassadors of Christ we will suffer, but our losses will be of a superficial, temporal nature. Our gain will be a new life—forgiveness of sin, an inheritance in heaven, and fellowship with God as we live here on earth.

Maria, the woman I told you about earlier, had to suffer for her faith too. Three months after her conversion I visited Quito again. When she learned I was there, she came to see me. I was shocked at her appearance. She obviously was happy, but her face was black-and-blue. Four of her front teeth were missing.

When I asked her what happened, she told me that she had given a speech at a major meeting of communist leaders in Ecuador, denouncing their beliefs and objectives and telling them of her new life in Christ. They were furious. Later, as she walked down a street, some party members beat her up, smashing her face into a light pole.

But Maria did not give up her faith. Assisted by evangelicals in Ecuador, she moved to a different location and continued to study the Bible. Eventually, some of her former comrades—key leaders in the communist movement in Ecuador—found her. Maria talked with them about her new beliefs. After convincing these leaders that they needed time to rest and think about what they were doing, she sent them—loaded with Bibles and Christian books—to her father's farm in a remote part of Ecuador. Because they were off studying this literature, a major Marxist revolution planned for Ecuador fizzled out.

Trouble and persecution continued to follow Maria. Whenever she found a job, her Marxist enemies telephoned her employer saying she was a troublemaker and telling lies about her until she was fired. Through it all, Maria has remained a strong Christian.

The problems an ambassador of Christ faces are not like the problems non-Christians face. There are many times when our problems are not produced by sin and selfishness. Instead, these troubles are a result of standing up for Christ and have a specific purpose.

Paul realized that as a minister of the Gospel—an ambassador—he was to be an example to others. He didn't want his actions to cause another person to stumble or harm the ministry of Christ in any way. Therefore, Paul tells us to take suffering and persecution with dignity so we don't create obstacles for anyone else.

While a young man, I did many things that I believe caused people to stumble. To impress my teenaged friends I acted indifferent during church services, talked rough, and bought myself a pipe. Nothing especially terrible, but my witness among those peers was ruined. When I realized this later, I was crushed. Humbled before God, I prayed the words of Psalm 69:6, asking the Lord to see that none of those who love Him would stumble because of me. The Lord forgave me, giving me peace about my past mistakes and the mistakes I surely will make in the future.

As ambassadors for Christ, we also take abuse so that we can be ready for future days of persecution. We don't want to react to persecution in our own strength, but in the Spirit, so that nothing we do will dishonor the Gospel of Christ. A Christian who lives in the power of the flesh rather than in the power of the indwelling Christ brings reproach to God. Paul wants to avoid this at all cost.

The apostle says we commend ourselves to God in every way—not just with words but with actions, even enduring suffering (2 Cor. 6:4). Paul maintained a balanced attitude in the midst of his suffering. He had patience and kindness for those who mistreated him, although a natural response would have been to seek revenge. Although his tormentors didn't deserve it, Paul loved them. Even though a lie might have delivered him from suffering, Paul spoke the truth. Every ambassador of Christ has the power, through the Holy Spirit, to maintain such an attitude in the midst of suffering.

Finally, we must remember the fruit that comes from suffering. Along with the sorrow of suffering, an ambassador of God's kingdom has the joy of the indwelling Christ—a joy that cannot be taken away. Paul can be joyful in the midst of his suffering because his joy is the result of sharing the eternal treasures of Christ with everyone—making them rich in Christ, as he is. Even if every material possession Paul had was taken away from him, he still would have *everything* because he is a son of God—an ambassador of Christ. When we possess that vision, the suffering we endure is worthwhile.

AN AMBASSADOR'S LOVE MAY NOT BE RETURNED

As an ambassador of Christ, Paul not only faced trouble and persecution from the heathen world around him, but also was troubled by a lack of love in the church. He writes to the church in Corinth:

> We have spoke freely to you, Corinthians, and opened wide our hearts to you. We are not withholding our affection from you, but you are withholding yours from us. As a fair exchange—I speak as to my children—open wide your hearts also (2 Cor. 6:11–13).

Even though the Corinthians were attacking Paul, he responds to them in love, without a hint of bitterness. Like a father, he says, "You can pressure me. You can accuse me. You can do whatever you like to me. But no one can lessen my love for you because you are my children; I brought you to Christ."

Then he pleads, "But please, love me a little too. I know you're playing games with me. You smile at me when I visit, but Titus has told me about the nasty things you say behind my back. Please open your heart to me. I need your love."

Everyone needs to be loved—not just by our spouse, parents, and children, but by our fellow believers. We were made for fellowship with one another. We are supposed to encourage, support, and love one another. This is the kind of love Paul asks the Corinthians to share with him.

Let's not put each other on. We need each other. Although some of us may be experiencing wonderful times when everything in life is great, other brothers and sisters may not be doing as well. They need our help and support. That's what the body of Christ is for.

As Christians we are to help each other, love each other, stand up for each other, pray for each other, cry with each other, and have fun with each other. The church isn't a club we join to make us look good; the church is a body of believers who love and care for one another. As Paul says, we need to have open, sincere hearts that are filled with Christ's love. Then we can be examples to others—ambassadors of Jesus Christ.

What a joy it is to be an ambassador for Jesus Christ! In my Bible, I've written a little poem that Corrie ten Boom recited:

When I enter that beautiful city,
and the saints all around me appear,
I hope that someone will tell me,
"It was you who invited me here."

FOR PERSONAL REFLECTION

Read 2 Corinthians 5:16–6:13.

1. "As human beings, we naturally have an ego-centered perspective of other human beings. That is, we perceive others in terms of their relationship to us." How do you perceive the people around you? Your family members? Your close friends? Your coworkers? Your acquaintances? Think of them by name.

2. "Until we come to Christ, we are rebels. We may be very nice, gentle, educated rebels; but we are rebels nonetheless. When we surrender to Jesus Christ, however, we are reconciled to God." How were you in rebellion against God? How has your life changed since you have been reconciled to Him? If you have not yet been reconciled to God—what's stopping you? Be reconciled today!

3. "No matter what our background, status, or natural sphere of influence, we are ambassadors of God." How does being Christ's ambassador shape your self-view and self-esteem? How does it shape your lifestyle? Your relationships?

4. "Everyone needs to be loved—not just by our spouse, parents, and children, but by our fellow believers." Why was Paul so passionate in asking for the Corinthians' love? In what ways do you need—and experience—the love of other believers?

FOR INTERACTIVE DISCUSSION

Read aloud 2 Corinthians 5:16–6:13.

1. Our view of Christ changes when we begin to live for Him. . . .
    We begin to see people in a different light as well." How does our
    perception of Jesus Christ change after we become Christians? How
    does our perception of other people change?

2. "Through the miraculous cleansing of Christ's blood, we become
    new creatures, we are reconciled to God." How does the wonder
    of reconciliation take place?

3. In spite of the dignity, honor, and respect shown ambassadors . . .
    it isn't all parties, speeches, and receptions." What are the responsi-
    bilities of an ambassador of Jesus Christ? What are the privileges?
    What are the risks?

4. "The church isn't a club we join to make us look good; the church
    is a body of believers who love and care for one another." How can
    the people in a church community open their hearts wider to each
    other? How does this expression of love fit into the ministry of
    reconciliation?

CHAPTER 12

Walking in Holiness

As ambassadors of Christ, we represent our Lord to the world. As God's children—His representatives on earth—God demands that we live holy lives. This point is communicated throughout Scripture, most notably when God states, "Be holy because I, the LORD your God, am holy" (Lev. 19:2).

Today, some Christians focus on the benefits of holiness, rather than on the reason God calls us to holiness. It's easy to think, *If we're holy, we'll be happy. If we're holy, we'll be successful. If we're holy, we'll be mature.*

All of these things may happen, but they have nothing to do with *why* God wants us to be holy.

God demands that His ambassadors live in holiness and purity because *He* is holy. If we want to have fellowship with God, we must be holy. We are not to seek holiness so we can be happy. We are not to seek holiness so we can further His kingdom. We are not to seek holiness so we can have power and authority in our lives. The only reason we should seek holiness is because God our Father is holy. The good things that result from holiness are an extra gift we receive from God, but they are not why we seek holiness.

How, then, do we become holy? We know that in and of ourselves we never can be truly holy. No matter how hard we strive for holiness, we'll always miss the mark. But when we finally stop pursuing holiness on our own terms and lay our efforts at the feet of Jesus, we can discover the true path to holiness. By bringing our shattered dreams and strivings to a loving God, we can be reconciled to Him. And once we have been reconciled, then—and only then—can we, too, be holy.

HOLINESS AND SIN CANNOT ABIDE TOGETHER

Paul explains God's definition of holiness and why He demands holy living:

> Do not be yoked together with unbelievers. For what do righteousness and wickedness have in common? Or what fellowship can light have with darkness? What harmony is there between Christ and Belial? What does a believer have in common with an unbeliever? What agreement is there between the temple of God and idols? For we are the temple of the living God. As God has said: "I will live with them and walk among them, and I will be their God and they will be my people" (2 Cor. 6:14–16).

Holiness can have nothing to do with that which is not holy. We can't pretend to be holy. We can't play games with sin or walk the narrow line between holiness and sin. We must be ruthless in our commitment to holiness. We must be willing to pay any price for holiness. We must not allow sin or insensitivity to the holiness of God to settle in our hearts.

Many times I have counseled men and women who have committed immoral acts. Often they say, "I don't know what happened! Everything was going fine, then all of a sudden . . . wham!" But a Christian who has been living a holy life in the power of the indwelling Christ cannot simply stumble into such sin. Satan can't just stick out his foot and trip holy Christians.

Immorality results when a Christian persists in entertaining unholy thoughts. Under this unhealthy influence, the will weakens and sensitivity to sin diminishes. Then, blinded by one's own passions, a Christian can fall into even the grossest sin.

We can't play games with holiness, thinking a little sin won't make any difference. If we belong to Him, we must crucify the flesh. We must say no to our sinful desires and say yes to God's desires for our lives. We must be holy.

Paul says the first requirement for holy living is to avoid being "yoked" with unbelievers. Other versions of the Bible use the term "mismated" (RSV). Throughout life we can choose to be joined with people who believe, or we can choose to be joined with people who don't believe. This is not just about joining a club or working together on a committee at the office. When we are "yoked together" with another person, we are in a mutually agreed upon, binding relationship that obligates us to that other person.

We can find several practical reasons for not being unequally yoked with unbelievers. In some parts of the world, animals are yoked together as a team to accomplish tasks that require greater strength than one animal alone can provide. People who harness animals in teams say it's important for the animals to be as equally matched in size, strength, and temperament as possible. If one animal is larger or stronger than the other, the team won't work well. If one animal is nervous or stubborn, it spoils the effectiveness of the calm, obedient animal. Paul is saying that when we are joined with unbelievers, trouble will ensue. So don't do it.

I believe it's important not to be yoked with unbelievers in at least two areas of life. The first is in marriage. The second is in business relationships.

A Christian never should go to the altar with a person whose commitment to Christ is uncertain. Christians who marry someone who is not a believer sin against God. And Christians who encourage other Christians to marry unbelievers also sin against God. A friend of mine used to say, "Anyone who marries an unbeliever has Satan for a father-in-law." That's a pretty horrible prospect!

As important as this teaching is, many Christians seem oblivious to it. When I was a young man, some of my friends, who were stronger Christians than I, married non-Christians. Because of their disobedience, their spiritual lives were wrecked. Of course, there's always a chance they will come back to God. But He is not fooled. We will reap what we have sown. If we sow in the flesh, we will reap the consequences of the flesh.

The same principle holds true in business. When Christians are yoked with unbelievers, the Christian may pull one way while the unbeliever pulls the other. The Christian may want to be honest in all areas while the unbeliever wants to alter the books to save on taxes.

I have counseled far too many Christians who ignored the Bible's warning and joined with unbelievers in marriage or business. They are paying dearly for their disobedience.

Why God Calls Us to Holiness

Being unequally yoked is painful. That alone should convince us that God's demand for holiness is reasonable. But Paul gives us five other reasons for God's call to holiness.

First, he asks how righteousness and iniquity can have anything to do with each other. A person who belongs to Christ wants to live a holy life because the holy God dwells within him or her. However, a person who doesn't belong to Christ lives in sin, not caring about holiness. Righteousness and iniquity don't mix; they cannot exist together.

Second, Paul asks how light and darkness can be together. Obviously, light and darkness are opposites. A Christian desires to walk in the light of the indwelling Christ. But someone who isn't a Christian prefers to walk in darkness. Like righteousness and iniquity, light and dark simply don't mix.

Third, Paul asks how Christ and Satan can have any agreement. They can't! Satan is Jesus Christ's greatest enemy. Every person who does not walk in the power of the indwelling Christ lives under the power and dominion of Satan. Therefore, we must make a radical decision to be holy. There is no middle ground.

Fourth, Paul asks what a believer and an unbeliever have in common. The truth is, not much. Their lack of communion brings conflict to the mismated pair and unhappiness to those around them.

Fifth, Paul says we are the temple of God. How can the temple of God defile itself with idols? How can we bring what is ungodly or unrighteous into the temple of God?

Certain laws cannot be changed. When we break those laws, we suffer the consequences. If we step out of a jetliner at thirty thousand feet without a parachute, we're not going to have a nice, soft landing. If we jump in front of a moving car, we're going to be hurt. God's laws are no different. If we disobey them, we will suffer the consequences. But God loves us dearly. He wants us to obey His laws so we can have intimate fellowship with Him.

Promises, Promises

If we obey God's call to holiness, we will receive His blessing. That's God's promise! God never asks us to do something that He will not enable us to do. When God calls, He always accompanies that call with a promise—a promise of His presence, His help, or His power. Paul lists seven promises that God will fulfill when we live holy lives through the power of the indwelling Christ.

> What agreement is there between the temple of God and idols? For we are the temple of the living God. As God has said: "I will live with them and walk among them, and I will be their God, and they will be my people."
>
> "Therefore come out from them and be separate, says the Lord. Touch no unclean thing, and I will receive you."
>
> "I will be a Father to you, and you will be my sons and daughters, says the Lord Almighty" (2 Cor. 6:16–7:1).

The first promise is that God dwells within us—He lives with us wherever we are.

The second promise is that God lives and walks among us. Notice that Paul uses the plural here, referring to the church—the body of Christ.

The third promise is that God will be our God. Paul reminds us that when we separate ourselves from what is improper and unrighteous, God will reveal Himself to us. We will feel and enjoy His presence.

The fourth promise is that we will be God's people. We aren't like the masses of the world; we are the people of God, the family of God. As His people, we have our identity with Him.

The fifth promise is preceded by God's call. He calls us to separate ourselves from past sins and everything in our lives that is unclean, improper, or sinful. Then He promises to receive us. What a promise! How beautiful it is to know that God receives us into His presence with open arms. I love to wake up in the morning and speak to my Heavenly Father, knowing that He waits for me to come to Him.

The sixth promise is that God will be a Father to us, an absolutely perfect Father. He will care for us, protect us, and love us. What more could He do for us?

The seventh promise is that God will confess us to the world as His sons and daughters. After promising to receive us and love us like a father, God promises even more. He pours His love upon us. He promises to honor us. There can be no greater honor than to stand before multitudes while God proclaims us His sons and daughters!

HOLY LIVING IS VICTORIOUS LIVING

After explaining God's promises to those who would live holy lives before Him, Paul gives a final exhortation:

> Since we have these promises, dear friends, let us purify ourselves from everything that contaminates body and spirit, perfecting holiness out of reverence for God (2 Cor. 7:1).

Once we realize the beautiful promises of God, isn't it reasonable that we should cleanse ourselves from anything that isn't holy? Why would we want to separate ourselves from all that pleases Him? Paul says, therefore, "let us purify ourselves from everything that contaminates body and spirit."

We cannot ignore the need for cleansing within the body of Christ. I have faced situations with my evangelistic team in which the work of God could not be accomplished due to sin within the leadership.

During one of our crusades in Central America, I sensed a separation from God in our work. I called the crusade committee together and said, "I am about to cancel this crusade because of unconfessed sin within the leadership. The Holy Spirit is grieved and we cannot go on."

Everyone was shocked. Finally, one of the members of the local committee spoke up. "I am living in adultery," he said. "The sin is with me."

We immediately gathered around the man to pray that he would be restored to fellowship with God. After he was restored, power and authority returned to the crusade. Many people became Christians.

We sometimes seem to think that only the physical, visible impurities of our lives need cleansing. Since the sins of the spirit are less visible, we tend to consider those particular sins less important. As a result, we may not be as diligent in cleansing ourselves of them. But God sees everything in perfect balance. He wants us to be holy and victorious in all areas of our lives.

Holiness isn't something we manufacture. Holiness isn't something we suddenly receive at a revival service. Holiness is a sign of maturity, an indication that we do, indeed, belong to God. It means that the Holy Spirit is working in our lives. It is a result of walking everywhere with a transparent conscience before God—in our places of business, while we drive our cars, while we shop for groceries, or while we play golf.

When I think of people who have lived holy, victorious lives, I think of Robert Murray M'Cheyne. Although he died at the young age of twenty-nine, he made a lasting impression on society.

M'Cheyne pursued the Lord's work with holiness, humility, and compassion. His faithful work paved the way for a great revival in Scotland. Just weeks before his death, he published *Daily Bread,* a Bible reading program to help his congregation know the Bible "in all its breadth."

The need for personal holiness before God so impressed him that he once wrote in a letter: "According to your holiness, so shall be your success. . . . A holy man is an awesome weapon in the hand of God."

Yes, holiness is an awesome weapon. Those who live in holiness before God are those who have fellowship with Him day by day. And those who walk with God, in the power of the indwelling Christ, will live in authentic victory!

FOR PERSONAL REFLECTION
_____

Read 2 Corinthians 6:14–7:1

1. "When we finally stop pursuing holiness on our own terms,
    and lay our efforts at the feet of Jesus, we can discover the true
    path to holiness." What does it mean to pursue holiness on your
    own terms? How is it different from a "ruthless commitment" to
    holiness?

2. "Throughout life we can choose to be joined with people who
    believe, or we can choose to be joined with people who don't
    believe." What "partnership" choices have you made in your life so
    far? How do these choices—and the ones you will make in the
    future—affect the holiness of your life?

3. "Once we realize the beautiful promises of God, isn't it reasonable
    that we should cleanse ourselves from anything that isn't holy?"
    How do these promises encourage and enable you to live a holy
    life?

4. "We sometimes seem to think that only the physical, visible
    impurities of our lives need cleansing." What areas of your life need
    cleansing today? How will you address these areas in light of all you
    have learned about living an authentic, victorious Christian life?

FOR INTERACTIVE DISCUSSION

Read 2 Corinthians 6:14–7:1

1. "Today, some Christians focus on the benefits of holiness rather than on the reason God calls us to holiness." What are the reasons God calls us to holy living?

2. "Paul is saying that when we are joined with unbelievers, trouble will arise. So don't do it." How is a "yoked together" relationship unique? What kind of trouble arises and why? What arguments does Paul use to plead with the believers not to be joined with unbelievers in this way?

3. "When God calls, He always accompanies that call with a promise—a promise of His presence, His help, or His power." What are the promises the Lord makes to those who are united to Him?

4. "Holiness isn't something we manufacture. . . . Holiness is a sign of maturity, an indication that we do, indeed, belong to God." How is holiness displayed in your life? How do you see it in the lives of others?

CORRESPONDENCE

Thank you for reading this book!

Every reader's experience with a particular book is different. So I hope I hear from you about what you found helpful, insightful, or thought-provoking. I also invite you to send me your specific questions or concerns—or tell me if you disagree with something I've said. That's OK too!

Here's how to reach me:

Luis Palau
P.O. Box 1173
Portland, OR 97207
USA
Telephone: (503) 614-1500
Fax: (503) 614-1599
lpea@palau.org
www.palau.org

FREE ONLINE RESOURCES

You'll find free excerpts from my newest books online at www.palau.org.

If you sign our www.palau.org guest book, my staff will be glad to send you a copy of my twenty-page message, *What Is a Real Christian?*, or a copy of my sixty-four-page study guide, *Going Forward with Jesus Christ*. Both are yours free for the asking.

While you're online, please take a minute to see what other readers have to say about this book. Then please feel free to add your own comments to our "Readers Say" page. You'll also find excerpts from published reviews and online discounts if you want to obtain additional copies of this book for individual friends or small groups.

Also be sure to check out our online "Faith Resource Center." You'll find a link right off our www.palau.org home page. There you can sign up to receive our free weekly "Healthy Habits for Spiritual Growth" devotional e-zine.

All of these resources are designed to encourage and inspire your faith.

God richly bless you in every area of your life as you seek His best!

ABOUT THE AUTHOR

The Wall Street Journal calls Luis Palau "the Billy Graham of everywhere." His popularity over the years in Latin America, the United Kingdom, Asia, and other parts of the world is rather remarkable.

During one evangelistic campaign, more than 528,000 people in London turned out to hear Luis Palau in person. He so captured the imagination of the British press that it started using his name as a synonym for enthusiasm.

A massive, mind-boggling crowd of 700,000 people gathered to hear Luis on Thanksgiving Sunday in Guatemala City a few years ago. Another 300,000 gathered to hear him in Managua, Nicaragua, last July.

Up to 140,000 are now turning out for his popular weekend evangelistic "festivals" in key cities across the United States.

AMERICAN BY CHOICE

Luis Palau stands out in this generation as a truly international Christian spokesman and leader. He's a third-generation transplanted European who grew up in the province of Buenos Aires, Argentina, and then chose to become an American citizen after completing the graduate course at Multnomah Biblical Seminary in Portland, Oregon.

Equally at ease in English and Spanish, Luis Palau commands audiences' attention wherever he goes. His solidly biblical, practical messages hit home in the minds and hearts of listeners.

"Sometimes it seems I have been preaching all my life," the sixty-seven-year-old evangelist says. "Actually, although I started preaching in Argentina as a teenager, it really wasn't until I was in my thirties that God opened the door for me to pursue full-time mass evangelism. And now in my sixties, He's opening up even bigger doors."

NEW INITIATIVES

Those bigger open doors include: publishing three evangelistic books for Doubleday, one of the largest secular publishers in New York; starting "Reaching Your World with Luis Palau," a new radio program already picked up by more than 850 affiliates; and launching Next Generation

Alliance®, a new ministry of the Luis Palau Evangelistic Association that actively assists younger evangelists.

"Billy Graham and others took the time to build into my life years ago. Thanks to their mentoring, I was spared a lot of unnecessary grief and dead ends," Luis says. "I'm now committed to coming alongside other younger, gifted evangelists."

Luis credits Graham, Dick Hillis, Ray Stedman, Keith Bentson, and other mentors for setting a positive example and warning him about the temptations that come with public ministry.

"So often, we don't like to talk about money, sexuality, pride, and the temptation to give up. But Scripture repeatedly says the older generation has a responsibility to exhort those who are younger," Luis says. "As a result, we often have to push ourselves outside our comfort zone to talk about such issues.

"The same is true when it comes to sharing the Good News with our loved ones, friends, and others. It's true, 'Actions speak loudest *with* words.'"

PLANTING ROOTS

Since moving to a new house four years ago, Luis and his wife, Pat, have made a point of spending time with their new neighbors. That includes accepting invitations to attend block parties, summer picnics, and other social events. "We're simply trying to follow the example of Jesus Christ, who took advantage of such opportunities to befriend everybody and share the Good News with them."

As part of their friendship evangelism efforts, Luis and Pat have made a point of praying by name for everyone in their neighborhood—and letting the word out slowly. "I mentioned something to one of my neighbors and the word got back to me at the Christmas party: 'We all heard that you're praying for us.' It's amazing. Seventy percent are unchurched. Nevertheless, they were all intrigued that we prayed for them.

"We've also made ourselves more and more available. When our neighbors' children have tickets or cookies for sale, we buy them every time. When they want to borrow chairs . . . we've become sort of a resource in the neighborhood.

"We used to have my secretary pick up our mail while we were traveling. She still does it some, but there's a lady across the street who says, 'Let me get your mail for you.' So we let her. All these little things build bridges."

Luis and Pat also invite their neighbors to join them on Sundays at a nearby church—the same church where they were married forty years ago. "It's great to have such deep roots in the community," Pat says, "especially since we spent most of our first fifteen years living in Mexico, Colombia, and Costa Rica." Since moving back to the States in the mid-1970s, Luis has gone on to minister in sixty-five more countries.

All four of Luis and Pat's sons and their families live in the Portland area as well. "I'm so grateful that each of our sons and daughters-in-law are dedicated to the Lord and have a heart for evangelism," Luis says. "The grandkids, well, they're getting there! I can't wait to see my great-grandkids receive the Lord someday."

LOOKING AHEAD

Luis Palau often jokes that he plans to serve the Lord until he's ninety-two.

Why ninety-two? "Well, when I was young, I read a biography of George Mueller, who had such a dynamic ministry to orphans in Bristol, England, during the nineteenth century.

"I lost my own dad when I was ten years old, so Mueller's story really made an impression on me. Especially the part that he kept right on serving until he died at age ninety-two. In fact, two Sundays before he died, he was in the pulpit preaching the Word. Why can't I aim for the same?"

What does Luis look forward to over the next twenty-five years?

"First, my dream is to see the Muslim world open up to the Gospel.

"Second, I'd love to have an opportunity to minister in every nation. We're already using literature, radio, television, and the Internet to reach tens of millions of people in 120 nations. But nothing can replace face-to-face ministry.

"Third, I'm praying for the Lord to raise up a new generation of godly evangelists who can saturate whole cities with the life-changing message of Jesus Christ.

"Fourth, I want to be faithful to the end."

LESSONS LEARNED

What is Luis Palau's secret?

"I remember talking with one of my mentors, Dick Hillis, after several nationally known Christian leaders fell into sin a few years ago. I asked him, 'What went wrong?' He thought about it for a while and then told me, 'I think you have to be careful to always stay in the Word. Read widely, sure. But never lose your hunger for the Scriptures.' I think he's right."

In addition to getting up early each morning to pray and study the Bible, Luis meets with a group of Christian CEOs on Wednesday mornings for additional prayer and accountability.

He also relies heavily on his ministry's board of directors and management team. "Most of them are younger than me," Luis admits. "Still, I've made a point of making myself accountable to them, listening to their counsel, and not always insisting that we do things the same old way. As a result, we've seen terrific results with our weekend festivals, our radio program, and several other new ministries."

REACHING YOUTH

So what's it like trying to preach to a crowd of 85,000 mostly young people after five back-to-back concerts?

"To be honest, I don't love the loud music," Luis says, "but I love the kids who love this kind of music. And we're seeing thousands of them commit their lives to Jesus Christ."

So is the day of "crusade" evangelism in stadiums and arenas now over?

"No, definitely not. But right now, festival evangelism has mass appeal. *Newsweek* and other media have reported extensively on this growing trend.

"Some have asked me if a festival is really 'crusade lite.' Actually, it's the opposite. We're going to large city parks where people already love to gather for citywide outdoor concerts. And we use contemporary Christian music, testimonies, and a clear-cut Gospel sermon to present the Gospel for five hours each night.

"It's no wonder so many people give their lives to Jesus Christ."

—*by David Sanford (originally published in* LifeWise *by Focus on the Family)*